"What do you ... young people are often ... they ask themselves.

What avenues are open? What would suit you? What qualifications are needed? A practical guide to the world of work.

Jenny Thewlis

Working On It: Thinking About Jobs

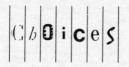

First published in Lions Choices 1989

Lions Choices is an imprint of
the Children's Division, part of
the Collins Publishing Group,
8 Grafton Street, London W1X 3LA

Copyright © Jenny Thewlis 1989
All rights reserved

Printed and bound in Great Britain by
William Collins Sons & Co. Ltd, Glasgow

Conditions of Sale

Contents

WHAT IS WORK?

What image does the word WORK conjure up for you?

- What your parents do?
- What people you know do for a living?
- What you do in school?
- What you hope to do when you leave school?

Work is one of those words which has a whole host of different meanings. One definition is 'effort directed to an end' which basically means doing something for a purpose. We mainly use the word 'work' nowadays to mean paid employment, but it can be applied to anything from washing-up to Maths homework.

This book is about the sort of things you need to consider when you are thinking about the work you want to do. It's not a careers book as such. If you want to know in detail about the different jobs available and the qualifications they require, I list books in the *Follow-Up* section of this book that will give you that information. This is really a pre-work book which I hope will get you thinking about some of the wider issues to do with work.

Work is going to be a big part of your life and for many young people it will determine how you see yourselves and how others see you, so it's worth thinking about it seriously.

One of the first questions people ask someone they've just met is 'What do you do?' by which they mean 'What work do you do?'

When people ask me what I do I say, 'I'm a teacher.' This immediately conjures up a certain image for most people. They will probably assume that I went to college or University, that I have a reasonable standard of living, that I have long holidays and it may even give them an idea of what newspaper I read and what my politics are. They would make different assumptions if I said I worked in Woolworths or that I was a company director.

A lot of women still say 'I don't work, I'm just a housewife.' Of course they don't mean that they sit round idly all day – washing, cleaning, cooking and child-care are definitely work and hard work. What they mean is that they are not doing paid work, so the questioner probably won't think it counts. Lots of women still feel apologetic about 'only' being a housewife. A few years ago a campaign called *Wages for Housework* was started by a group of women who felt that the work of women in the home should be properly recognised.

We tend to forget that many women actually do two jobs – a paid job and housework and child-care. Not many men do that!

The funny thing is that if you look after someone else's house or kids then it *is* seen as work – you are 'a cleaner' or 'a nanny'. If you cook someone else's meals for them, you are 'a cook'.

Although people tend to define themselves by their work, paid work is often not the most important activity in their lives. There's an old saying that some people work to live and others live to work.

For people who 'work to live', work is an unavoidable necessity to provide the money needed to live on. They may be people with boring, repetitive jobs such as factory work, who walk away at the end of the day to get on with their 'real' lives, or they may be people whose main interest – whether it's going to discos, gardening, playing chess, making models, political activity – has nothing to do with their paid work.

For people who 'live to work', work *is* their main interest in life. You often hear people described as being 'married to their work'. This may be because the work itself is interesting and rewarding: doing scientific research, playing in a band, being a TV producer. It may be that they are so busy making money that they don't have time for anything else, like some people working in the Stock Exchange, or it may be that the rest of their life is lonely and miserable and even a dull job gives them contact with other people and something to talk about.

There is a third group, and that's the people who don't work at all. It may be because they are unemployed in which case they are probably working hard looking for work and still define themselves in terms of their work. ('I'm a painter-decorator'; 'I'm a machinist.') It may be that they are retired or it may be that they don't actually want to work. It can also be that they are so wealthy that they don't have to work.

But whatever the case, in work or out of it, there's no getting away from the fact that work is central to most people's lives.

But work is not something which is the same for everyone. It has changed through history, it is often different depending on whether you are a man or a woman, black or white, rich or poor.

Work can be indoors or outdoors, solitary or with hundreds of other people, paid or unpaid. It's important that you should understand this before you look at your own working life.

A POTTED HISTORY OF WORK

Work has always been what most people needed to do in order to live. In early times people had to work at hunting animals and gathering roots and berries. As agriculture developed that became the main form of work. People worked to feed and clothe themselves, at first directly from what they produced, later through trade as well. Men and women did different kinds of work but together it ensured the survival of the family or the tribe. This is still the way of life for many people in the world today.

But societies don't stand still. As people's way of life developed and became more complicated, different sorts of work evolved. One of the main changes came when certain powerful people realised that they could force others to work for them. This was what slavery was all about and serfdom, too, during the Middle Ages. Not all work developed in this way of course. There were merchants and craftsmen who had things that others wanted to buy, but most people only had their labour to sell. They worked as farm hands, builders, miners or servants, and later on in factories, on the roads and railways and in offices and shops. In return for their work they were paid a wage. By the end of the last century, society in Britain was divided into three main classes – the upper class and the aristocracy who owned the land; the middle class, who were merchants, bankers and managers; and the working class, who made up the majority of the population.

For most people there was no choice of job. Working life began at thirteen and lasted until death, which was likely to be before fifty. In the cotton industry in Lancashire boys of eleven could be employed for five hours a day as half-timers. This meant getting up at five in the morning to work in the mills before going to school in the afternoon. Girls of twelve or thirteen would be working in service as maids in wealthy households getting up at five as well to clean grates and lay fires.

In a book called *Child Slaves of Britain* written in 1905 Robert Sherard describes piece work done by children at home:

> *One penny a day* (that's less than half a pence) *can be gained by a child in bending the tin clasps around safety pins . . . At*

wrapping up hair pins in paper, ten to a paper with one outside to hold the package together . . . as much as 2¼d (about one pence) can be earned by four children in a couple of days.

Accounts like this shocked people, as had the observations of Charles Booth, a Victorian businessman who spent many years studying and writing about poverty. People were also shocked by the novels of Charles Dickens but little was done to alter the appalling conditions under which children toiled.

Jobs were dangerous too. There were no safety regulations or protective clothing. Between 1875 and 1899, 12,870 men were killed working on the railways and over 68,000 injured. A goods guard killed while shunting had been on duty for over twenty-two hours. And the pay for working in such conditions? In 1907 it was less than a pound a week.

In 1926 boys were still allowed to go down the mines at fourteen – at a time when a miner was killed every five hours and five maimed every ten minutes! And it wasn't just men and boys who suffered danger at work. Women working in places like match factories or for hatters were prey to fatal industrial diseases.

Social reformers and workers themselves struggled to improve working conditions. The Trades Unions were formed to protect men and women from being overworked and underpaid and to try to improve the quality of people's working lives. They are still working to achieve these aims today, as we'll see later in this book. Charitable organisations were set up to help people, while in parliament acts were passed to remedy some of the worst aspects of work. The Labour Party was established to campaign for better conditions and to give the working class a voice.

Of course, times have changed and work has changed. In 1830 seven out of ten people in Britain worked in agriculture but by 1930 over half the population worked in manufacturing. This has changed again so that today only one in four works in manufacturing and the majority work in the new service industries (eg banking, finance, insurance, transport, entertainment).

The types of job which were on offer to your parents are not all going to be on offer to you. But you will have new work possibilities that your parents and certainly your grandparents could not have imagined. Whole new areas of work – the leisure industry, the service industries, the microtechnology industries are rapidly expanding.

One of the main reasons for this change is the development of machinery to take the place of people. There are car factories now where all the work is done by robots with only a handful of human supervisors, whereas twenty years ago there would have been hundreds of workers on the assembly line. The decline in heavy industry and the replacing of people by machines has meant that less labour is needed. There are fewer jobs and more unemployment. In the 1950s only 300,000 were unemployed; today the figure is around 3½ million – a harsh fact that you shouldn't forget when thinking about work possibilities.

But let's move on to a rather more cheerful thought. Mechanisation also means that people today have more free time – longer holidays and shorter working weeks – than they used to. People who retire from work can, hopefully, look forward to another ten or twenty years of life. A hundred years ago they would probably have died 'in harness'.

Free time or leisure is time that is your own, not the firm's and historically it is quite a novelty for most people. Of course there have always been people with leisure, those who could afford to play while others worked. One sociologist referred to them as 'the leisured class' to distinguish them from the working class. But as leisure time has expanded it has also generated its own industry. The leisure industry provides leisure activities from fruit machines to football matches, from night clubs to symphony concerts.

The leisure industry is part of the service industry, the fastest growing sector of the economy. In 1986 the total employed in service industries was 14,495,000 as opposed to 11,627,000 in 1971. Just think of some of the areas related to it – banking and finance, transport, communications, travel agents, record companies, advertising, video making, all sorts of catering, snooker halls, discos . . . all of them needing workers.

There's another consideration about leisure that's really a bit of a contradiction but worth thinking about. That is, that one person's leisure activity can be another person's work. Take the following:

> professional football players
> professional snooker players
> chat show hosts
> professional musicians
> artists
> dressmakers
> painters and decorators
> gardeners
> cooks

All of these are paid jobs but they are also things that a lot of people do just for fun. You can probably think of several other examples. Of course they might stop being fun if you had to do them all day every day, but it's another aspect of the world of work that you need to take on board.

Another side of the service industry, but a very different one, is Public Service. This includes all those areas which are needed in a civilised and caring society, but which don't make a profit and have to be paid for out of money raised by rates and taxes. Hospitals, libraries, street cleaning, social services, education, the police are just some of them. People often choose to work in these areas because they feel they are doing some good for society.

VOLUNTARY WORK

Some people want to do something to help others who are disadvantaged in some way. Because this sort of work is not usually well paid, if paid at all, a whole field of voluntary work has grown up. You can volunteer:

    to visit people in prison
    to help on hospital wards
    to teach people to read
    to shop for housebound old people
    to take mentally handicapped
      children swimming
    to reclaim ponds . . .

The list is endless.

Some people would argue, and I'd be one of them, that in a really civilised society the government should be prepared to pay for this kind of work and not rely on people's good will. After all, there are millions of people unemployed. If they were paid to work as hospital cleaners or in nature conservancy, wouldn't it be better all round? There's a lot of evidence to show that those people in work would not mind paying a bit extra on their taxes to make sure that we have decent hospitals and clean and pleasant environments. Work is socially important as well as economically important, after all.

Well, I've whistled through the history, the sociology and the economics of work. Where does it all leave you? You are the person that all this is about. You are going to have to make the decisions about your place in the labour market. I call it the labour market because when it comes down to it that is still what work is about – selling your labour. It might be physical or intellectual but whether you are going to be a labourer, an office worker or a research chemist, you are still selling.

Not all labour is given the same value. In Britain women's labour is worth less than men's – the average gross weekly wage for a female manual worker is still only 62% of a man's.

People in the North of England earn less than those in the South. Black people on average earn less than white. Some people don't earn anything at all. Some people earn lots of money without working. So let's pull all this together. Here's a summary of things you need to bear in mind when thinking about work. We'll look at most of them in more detail later in the book.

WHAT DO YOU ENJOY DOING?

Think of all the things you are interested in both in school and out. Think of all the things you don't like doing as well. If you hate Maths you're not likely to enjoy being an accountant. If you hate getting dirty you won't want to be a motor mechanic. If you enjoy books you might want to be a librarian. It doesn't matter at this stage if you haven't got the foggiest idea of what you want to be.

WHAT HAVE YOU GOT TO SELL?

This might sound rather mercenary, but as we've seen, it's the way of the world. Still, it's nicer to think of it as what you've got to offer. What are your personal qualities? Are you patient, impulsive, quiet, extrovert . . .? Think of your good sides and your bad sides.

What qualifications do you think you'll have to offer? A degree? GCSEs? Vocational qualifications?

What other skills or interests have you got to offer? Good with your hands? Play sports? Belong to a drama club?

There are all sorts of things that can sell you to an employer and they're not always the obvious ones like qualifications.

WHAT DO YOU NEED TO REMEMBER

• If you are a woman or a member of an ethnic minority, you are still at a disadvantage in the job market. In spite of legislation, you are likely to earn less and have less chance of promotion.

• Where you live (in the town or in the country, in the North of Britain or the South) will affect your job prospects.

• The labour market is changing all the time. A job now is not likely to be a job for life in the way it was for your grandparents or even your parents. Then, chances were that people went into a firm or factory at fifteen and emerged at sixty proudly clutching a gold watch for long and faithful service! Now the pace of change is so fast (as a result of new technology and the decline of traditional occupations) that there's no real way of knowing what the world of work will be like in twenty years' time. Lots more people may work from home using computer terminals and fax machines. Factory work may have disappeared entirely as people are replaced by machines. The working week may only be four days long. In school a favourite essay title is *Imagine Life in the Year 2020* and it's something you need to be able to try to do when you're thinking about work – and about leisure, because there will be changes there too.

• It's as important to think about the quality of your life away from work as about your life at work. The quality of life is made up of all sorts of different things and work is just one of them!

WHO AM I AND WHAT CAN I DO?

The trouble with having to think about work and the future at your age is that you often aren't really sure who you are, let alone what you want to be. You are living through a time of change, when your body and mind are starting to make the shift from childhood into adulthood. It's a time when you often feel neither one thing nor the other. One day you may be fooling around like an eight-year-old, the next, demanding that your parents treat you like an adult and let you go to all night parties or on holiday with your friends.

It's a time of life when you begin to establish an identity or personality which will be yours for the rest of your life.

Psychologists often talk about an adolescent identity crisis because adolescence is a time of such upheaval and change.

It's a time when you want to test the limits that adults set you and establish your independence, but when it's also important to be one of the gang and identified by the sort of clothes you wear or the music you listen to.

On the one hand you may become very self-centred, worrying about how others see you, spending ages examining yourself in the mirror and in your mind . . .

On the other hand you may start to develop an interest in wider issues, in the world around you, and begin to care passionately about nuclear war, vivisection or famine.

There are other complications to being an adolescent. It's the time when you begin to develop your sexuality, when you experiment with relationships and fall in love for the first time. It's a time when your emotions are like a seesaw – you can be happy and bubbling one minute, sulky and withdrawn the next.

It's an age of possibilities and uncertainties that everyone has been through, although it's often hard to imagine your teachers or parents having a crush on a pop star, or locking themselves in their rooms and sulking for hours, however often they assure you that they were young once!

In fact, one of the most common feelings in adolescence is that no-one understands you. This often comes about because you don't really understand yourself and the rapid changes that are taking place in you.

Let's look at some of the ways you can start to understand more about yourself and what makes you tick. By the time you reach adolescence there have already been lots of influences which have helped shape how you are so far:

JEANETTE (fifteen)

My best quality is that I'm sympathetic. When my mates have got problems they always come to me. If my brother and his girlfriend have an argument they tell me about it and ask me to choose the right side. He always comes to me to ask what he should wear if he's going out – things like that.

My bad side is that I get angry quickly. I'm easy to annoy, as well.

I'd like to be a secretary or a clerk. I think an employer would like me to be able to type, but otherwise they'd choose by personality – the way you look, the way you dress, whether you get on with people.

YOUR FAMILY

For better or worse, your family is perhaps the most important shaper of you as a young person, and your parents are usually the people who do most of the shaping. Some of this is obvious and easy to see – they set standards for your behaviour, for example, but some of it is less obvious, in fact invisible, and takes place in what psychologists call your unconscious. Sigmund Freud, a famous psychologist working at the beginning of this century, wrote a great deal about the relationship between children and their parents and the ways in which these influence people's personalities.

So here are some family influences. Think about how they apply to your own upbringing. Perhaps you can put your parents on the spot about some of them!

The size and shape of your family

This might not seem a particularly obvious influence at first sight but things like:

- whether you have any brothers and sisters
- where you come in the family – youngest? oldest? in between?
- whether you are brought up by one parent, or two, or someone else
- Whether your grandparents or other relatives live with you

can all make a difference to how you grow up.

If you are the oldest child in your family you will be treated differently, although this probably won't be deliberate on the part of your parents – it's one of those unconscious influences we were talking about.

If you have been brought up with two parents you will turn out differently than if you were brought up by one.

Grandparents sometimes spoil you and let you get away with things that your parents might not!

How you have been conditioned by your family

Conditioning is another word for training. It applies to how you behave and how you think. All sorts of factors help condition us. These are some of the questions to ask about the way you have been conditioned by your family, especially your parents:

- Were you played with and talked to a lot when you were a baby?
- Did you get lots of cuddles?
- How were you toilet trained? (Yes, this really can affect your personality!)
- Were boys and girls treated differently in the family?
- What sort of behaviour was expected from you?

- What sort of things were you punished or rewarded for?
- Who were you allowed to play with?
- How do your parents want you to turn out?
- What sort of example did your parents set?

Parents are usually the first role-models children have for how adults behave. If your mother stayed at home and your father went out to work, if your mother always did the cooking and cleaning and your father always changed the plugs and fixed the car, if your mother always spoiled you and your father always punished you, then you will have been shaped very differently than if the opposite had been true.

Of course things don't happen as neatly as this, and parental stereotypes aren't usually so rigid. Although it may look as if you start as a blob which is then shaped by others, from the moment you are born you are interacting with people around you, so that even as a very tiny infant you influence the way others behave towards you. As you grow older and develop more self-control you can do this quite consciously. It's an old chestnut that if you're nice to people then they'll be nice to you, but that's the sort of thing I mean.

Let's leave the family for a bit and move on to the next shaper that you will encounter.

CORETTA (sixteen)

The best thing about me is that I'm very friendly – I can get on with anyone if I want to. I can hold back my temper, too.

One thing that might offend people is that I'm really upfront. I come right out and say what I mean.

I'd like to work looking after children – child-minding or in a nursery. I can understand children, I know how to talk to them and I'm very caring. I'll do a two year course and at the end I'll get a certificate. It means I'm a responsible person and qualified to look after children.

SCHOOL

School is quite a deliberate influence. One of the jobs of the education system is to turn out the sort of young people that a particular society needs. This means making sure that they have the skills and attitudes that are valued in that society. This process is called socialisation.

Socialisation starts at primary school. Different types of teaching methods influence how children develop. For example, if you were allowed to play a lot and discover things for yourself at primary school the chances are that you will have a different attitude to learning than someone who was made to sit at a desk and recite tables.

When you move to secondary school all sorts of factors will influence you. For example:

- Whether you go to a comprehensive or a selective school
- whether you are educated privately
- whether you are taught in mixed ability groups or whether you are streamed
- if the school is single sex or mixed
- if it is mixed, do both sexes get an equal chance to take all subjects or are boys discouraged from joining typing classes while girls are made unwelcome in metal work?
- whether your teachers stand at the front of the class and dictate notes to you or whether you work in groups on different projects
- how much say you have in the running of the school
- what sorts of rewards and punishments there are . . .

I'm sure you can think of lots more points which affect you, not least whether you enjoy school or can't wait to leave.

TIM (fourteen)

My personality's OK. I mix with lots of different people and I make mates very easily. I think I'm alright really. I get on well with people of my own age, but not older people like my parents.

My bad side is that I'm normally lazy and can't be bothered to do anything. I hope to get at least five GCSEs and then go on to Art College at sixteen to do a B.Tech. course in Graphic Design. Then I'd like to work in advertising. It's well paid. I'll need to stop being so lazy and work harder, though.

FRIENDS AND PEERS

One of the chief influences on you, both in school and out, are your friends. They, and other young people of similar age and background, are sometimes referred to as your peer group, and they play an important part in shaping you as a person.

Remember when you were little and had a different best friend every day depending on who shared their sweets with you at playtime? Well, by now you should be choosing your friends in a rather more thoughtful way. If you think about

what you like about your best friend you might
come up with:
- I can confide in her/him
- we've got the same sense of humour
- I respect her/his opinions
- She/he's really generous
- we like the same music, books,
  TV programmes
- we both belong to CND

A friend is someone you feel closer to, and
have more in common with, than the rest of your
peer group. What they think and what they say
can influence you deeply.

A group of friends who hang out together
often see themselves as a gang. A gang can be just
a bunch of mates who spend most of their spare
time together and enjoy doing the same things,
or it can be a much more intense group with its
own rules, ways of dressing and slang.

Each generation produces its own particular
styles and forms of gangs – Teddy boys, mods,
rockers, skinheads, punks, hippies, greasers . . .
Not all young people throw themselves whole-
heartedly into a particular style but most are
influenced to some extent.

Being part of an identifiable group like this
provides a ready made image, a sort of identi-kit
personality which gives a feeling of belonging.

These groups often have their own sets of

values. Sometimes they can be nice but sometimes really nasty – many skinheads are racists, some groups go in for violent behaviour. Most gangs tend to be predominantly boys but some of the gang identity rubs off on to girls as well. Overall it seems to be boys who most need to slip on the identi-kit provided by a group or gang.

One of the aims of many such groups is to behave in a way which their members know their parents won't approve of. It's part of the process of separating yourself from your parents' influence, but by joining a group, you get shaped by the group's influence. It's a stage that young people usually grow out of, but it can seem very important at the time.

The last major shaper of you is society itself. The influences here are a bit harder to untangle but it's worth a try.

SOCIETY

First there are the expectations of society. These would be different if you were a young person in Russia or China, or if you were growing up in New Guinea. Adolescents in some parts of the world are expected to be full working members of their community and in other parts of the world are still considered to be children.

Then there's social class – your attitudes and outlook are greatly conditioned by whether you are working class, middle class or upper class.

Next, what about gender? Men and women, girls and boys, are still treated very differently in our society.

Where you live can help shape you as a person too. If you are brought up in a country village or on a farm you will be a different sort of person to someone brought up in the heart of the inner city.

The influence of the media is a powerful identity shaper – especially TV and newspapers, but also pop music. They all present a particular version of what young people are, and how they should behave. They also put a particular view of the world inside your head which it is often difficult to resist. Other things that can affect you deeply and help shape your ideas are films, music and, especially, books.

So who you are today is a result of all the things we've just looked at. You are an individual with a history and a future, but you're also a member of a family, of a peer group and of society as a whole, and all these things influence you whether you realise it consciously or not. But you in your turn influence them. You're not just a smooth piece of wax on which everyone else stamps an impression.

Before you start thinking about your future you need to sit down and take a long hard look at the self which has been shaped so far.

A PICTURE OF YOU

Let's get on with it then. By the end of this section you should begin to form a pretty clear picture of yourself – your likes and dislikes, strengths and weaknesses. It's useful to start by thinking of what you like and don't like about yourself and to check this with someone else. If you both agree, then you're off to a good start.

Look at this list and see how many of these qualities – or their opposites – apply to you:

adventurous	flexible
assertive	generous
calm	good-tempered
careful	hard-working
competent	honest
concerned	humorous
conscientious	imaginative
cooperative	loyal
curious	open-minded
dependable	patient
easy-going	persevering
enthusiastic	polite

punctual
questioning
reliable
resourceful
self-confident

sincere
sympathetic
tidy
tolerant

Obviously if you were all of these things you'd be too good to be true, and if you were none of them then you'd be a very inadequate and unpleasant person. Most of us have a mixture of good and not-so-good qualities but being able to recognise our own strengths and weaknesses is one way of knowing ourselves better.

Other things to bear in mind are your likes and dislikes. I don't mean whether you hate spiders or love hamburgers, but the sort of things that throw some light on your character.

Try sorting these out into likes and dislikes:

getting up early
meeting people
doing puzzles
travelling
tidying your room
going to parties
the countryside

making things
being alone
having responsibility
talking and arguing
dressing up
going to school

There are all sorts of other things which you could include and try out on your friends.

Let's go back to the things you like and don't like about yourself. It's quite hard to be honest with yourself about this because no one likes to admit to their bad qualities. You may be lazy, mean, spiteful some of the time but kind, generous and hard-working at others.

How you see yourself is known as your self-image.

If you are lucky you will have a positive self-image – you will be confident, out-going, sure of yourself, pleased with the way you look and behave, happy with your family and friends and sure that people like you.

A negative self-image means that you think poorly of yourself, feel that you compare badly with those around you, have nothing to offer and no abilities and feel that nobody likes you. Do you feel this applies to you? Well, so do most teenagers.

Adolescence is a time of great uncertainty about identity and young people tend to spend time thinking about what's wrong with them, rather than what's right.

If you're thinking negatively you'll say:

- they'll never choose me
- I could never do that
- I'm not intelligent enough, attractive enough, talented enough . . .
- you're only saying that . . .

If you're thinking positively you'll say:
- I've got as good a chance as the next person
- I can always have a go
- I'm reasonably intelligent, attractive, talented . . .
- Thanks for recognising my good qualities.

Let's face it, if you were interviewing two young people for a job, one negative, one positive, which would you choose?

Your personal qualities, your likes and dislikes, your abilities and aptitudes all have an influence on what sort of work you might be good at as well as what you might like to do.

Some things are fairly obvious. If you are good at technical subjects at school and interested in cars or motorbikes and enjoy working with your hands, then you might very well want to be a mechanic.

If you enjoy maths and computer work, but don't much care for mixing with other people, then a job as a systems analyst or a computer programmer might suit you.

On the other hand you might really enjoy meeting people and be quite good at English and Business Studies in which case a job in a bank or estate agents, or perhaps as a receptionist or personal assistant in an office could appeal to you.

If you are interested in social studies and

the humanities and want a job where you can do something to help others, then some kind of social or charity work will interest you.

Very often we let what we are good at at school dictate what sort of job we do without really weighing up the other factors that we've been talking about. We can easily get pigeon-holed into science, arts, technical subjects without realising that we can combine them, or even that they might not be the sort of thing we want to do at all – we just don't know the alternatives. For example, if you are really interested in science but enjoy English as well, you could become a scientific journalist. Or if you're keen on Technology and good at languages, you could be a technical translator.

One thing that you need to remember is that there is really no such thing as men's work and women's work – and that's official and backed up by law. We'll look at this in more detail in the last chapter, but it's something you need to bear in mind when thinking about a job. Don't let people put you off what you are really interested in doing by saying 'it's a hard job for a girl, you know' or 'boys don't really understand babies in the same way as girls' etc. If you're a girl who wants to be a car mechanic or a boy who wants to be a nurse, go for it! The number of women doing technical and engineering work,

RICKY (sixteen)

My good qualities? I can grasp new things quickly. I can adapt to things and get used to people real quick – like fit in with anyone. I don't make trouble and I'm quiet most of the time. I'm hard-working when I'm in the mood.

Bad points? I'm lazy, man. I have to be pushed to work. If people say it's up to you, you don't have to work if you don't want to, I won't. I'm just lazy. I prefer sleeping, lying in bed. I'm going to have to change when I go to work or I'll get the sack.

I want to do something like computing or electronics 'cos I reckon that's the future. I could be working in an office or factory that puts together stereos, things like that. I'd prefer to work in an office, but not a shirt, tie and suit sort.

I'm going to do a YT Scheme in Information Technology. I'll be a trainee, I'll have to get used to the people who are training me and for the first couple of months I'll have to work hard to try and fit in with it and adapt to different things.

driving buses and trains, working as carpenters and painters is growing every day. There's also been a rise in the numbers of men working in nursing, in child-care and in other traditionally 'female' areas.

THE MAJOR AREAS OF WORK

Here's a quick rundown on some of the major areas of work and the sort of qualities and abilities you might need if you are interested in working in them.

Obviously, as a school leaver you'll start at the bottom. With a college or university qualification you'll start a bit higher up the ladder, but you will need a lot of the same qualities.

Office Work
You need to be:

a good and efficient organiser
neat and methodical
good at spelling and punctuation
good with figures
able to get on with people
happy with a routine

Creative Work
You need to be:

imaginative and articulate

artistic
flexible
happy working under pressure

Technical and Scientific Work
You need to be:
interested in problem solving
able to work in a team
practical and methodical
good with calculations

Caring Work
You need to be:
interested in people and their problems
prepared to work for lowish wages
sympathetic but firm-minded
able to cope with emergencies

Construction Work
You need to be:
happy working outdoors
physically fit
good with your hands
able to take orders
able to work as part of a team

Service Work (shops, catering etc)
You need to be:
able to get on with people

willing to stand on your feet all day
prepared to wear some sort of uniform
good with figures
honest and reliable

These are only some of the main areas of work. I'm sure that you can think of others and also now begin to think of the sort of skills and qualities those areas require. Some qualities are common to all areas: reliability, honesty, perseverance and a good temper, are required in every walk of life. Skills that you learn in one area can be applied to another, as well. These are called 'transferable skills'.

Now you've got an idea of yourself and perhaps a rough idea of what you might want to do when you reach school leaving age. In the next chapter we'll look at some of the nitty-gritty decisions that have to be made as you decide on your future.

HOW DO I DECIDE?

So now you have a reasonably objective picture of yourself – that is, you can see yourself as others see you, as well as being able to look at your own qualities in a balanced sort of way.

What's the next step? You've examined who you are and what you're able to offer. Now you need to look at what you want to do.

Only a very few young people have an absolutely clear idea of what they want from an early age. Sometimes they have a definite talent, for music or art or swimming for example, and train that talent, sometimes from infancy. An article in *The Observer* newspaper (10.1.88) describes eleven-year-old James Schroder who:

> is about to hold his first art exhibition in a professional gallery, having gained an

A grade at 'O' level when he was ten . . . James, from Waterlooville, Hampshire, said: 'I don't want to be an ordinary painter. I want to be a great artist.'

You've probably also seen pictures of very young children playing the violin or other musical instruments and read of young people who are geniuses with computers.

Sometimes young people are expected to follow in the family business, working in a shop or a small family firm, or to follow the same career pattern as their parents – as a doctor or a lawyer for example.

Occasionally you find young people who have already developed a sense of vocation. This means that they feel called to do something, usually involving caring for other people, such as nursing or working in Third World countries, or teaching.

Then there's ambition. This is a bit different to a vocation, because it might be that you want to be a millionaire by the time you are twenty-five! But it could also mean that you want to be the leader of the Labour Party or a professional snooker player. In any case if you have a strong enough sense of ambition it will control the path that you take in your working life.

None of these apply to you? Don't worry.

Most young people have only a very general idea of what they want to do. Sometimes this is more negative than positive:

- I don't want to work in an office
- I don't want a boss breathing down my neck
- I don't want to have to clock in every day

Or else it may be rather vague but have some sort of focus:

- I want an outdoor job
- I want to work with people
- I want to do something practical.

Your self-examination in the last chapter should have given you a more solid idea of what you like and don't like, can and can't do.

Let's look now at some of the choices that you will need to make.

One basic choice is – do you want a job or a career?

Although in certain circumstances a job may lead to a career, they are two very different kettles of fish. Once you have made that decision all sorts of other decisions fall into place. How do other people manage it?

SUSAN, SEAN, AYESHA AND WINSTON

Susan, Sean, Ayesha and Winston all attended the same comprehensive school in a large town. They have gone through the school in the same tutor group even though, by the time they reached the fifth form, they were often in separate subject groups. They have been given lots of advice about their future, from the school's careers teacher and the Careers Officer as well as from their own tutor. By the end of the fifth year they have each taken some decisions about the way ahead for them.

These decisions revolved around whether to stay on at school or to leave and start work; whether to opt for school or college; whether to try for qualifications or not; whether to aim for a career or settle for a job. Let's look now at where these four people have got to one year on, and what motivated them to take the decisions that they did.

SEAN is now working as a scaffolder. He gets good money but the work is potentially dangerous and he hasn't had a proper training. Sean never really liked school. He saw it as somewhere to meet his mates and have a laugh – usually at the expense of some poor teacher. He was never really bad, just bored. His older brothers were all working on building sites bringing home plenty of money, free to come and go as they liked. Sean never considered staying on at school or going to college. He left school as soon as he could, without taking any GCSEs – although his teachers had always said that if only he'd put in some effort he could have passed Craft, Design and Technology, and perhaps English and Maths as well. The trouble was, Sean helped out in a local shop in the evening and on Saturday so there was never any time for homework, and anyway he preferred watching videos when he came in from work.

SUSAN is studying Biology, Chemistry and Physics at 'A' level and has a place in medical school waiting for her if she passes her exams. She's known from early on that she wants to be a doctor. So while her friends were taking Saturday jobs and going clubbing in the evenings, Susan concentrated on passing her GCSEs. She did well, especially in science subjects and so was able to continue with the subjects she already knew would qualify her for a place in medical school. Susan is happy to stay on at school. She has lots of friends there and is well liked by the staff. She enjoyed the clubs and activities provided by the school and always helps with the lighting in school plays. By the end of her first year in the sixth form she is made a senior prefect.

AYESHA had been one of Susan's best friends in the fifth form, but she decided to continue her studies at the local college of Further Education. Here she is studying for a BTEC (Business and Technical Education Council) National Award in Computer Studies. Ayesha's parents would have liked her to stay on at school but she convinced them that the facilities that the college had to offer were much more up-to-date and she would have more access to them than she would have to the school computers. What also appealed to Ayesha about college was the fact that it would give her more freedom and independence than she had at school. She felt that she had outgrown school, even though she knew that in the sixth form she would no longer have to wear school uniform, and would be able to leave the premises during free periods.

WINSTON has also been a good friend of Susan's and Ayesha's. He took GCSEs in English and Art but hadn't made up his mind what to do. He'd thought of going to college to train to be a carpenter – his mum was keen on him carrying on with some sort of education, but he'd left it too late to apply and all the places on the courses he wanted were taken. He didn't want to stay on at school, he'd had enough of it, and anyway there wasn't a satisfactory course available for him and he certainly didn't want the hassle of re-sitting exams. The Careers teacher had talked about YTS (Youth Training Schemes) and the Careers Officer had been plugging them hard. Winston thought that they seemed reasonable – he'd get some money in his pocket and some training as well. He signed on for a course which taught carpentry, painting and decorating and found himself placed with a local firm. It didn't take him long to pick up the skills, he'd been good at Woodwork at school and had often done odd jobs around the house. By the end of the first year on the scheme Winston decides that he could make more money working for himself.

JOB OR CAREER?

Let's go back to that basic decision – a job or a career – and look at these four young people's choices in the light of it.

Sean and Winston chose jobs, Susan and Ayesha careers – all mean work of course, so what's the difference?

A job can be any sort of work, from unskilled

labouring through to being a skilled technician. There are a lot of people who argue that being a wife and mother is also a job, even though it is unpaid!

There are many jobs you can do that require no formal qualifications, where the weekly wage is quite good. Shop work and factory work are obvious examples. On the other hand, certain jobs carry considerable responsibility (eg being a postal worker; working as a nursing auxiliary), while others need a considerable amount of training, either on the job or at college (eg electrician, information processor). Some jobs may lead to a career, such as from office junior, through various stages of responsibility, to office manager.

Basically though, there are two main types of job:

- *Dead end jobs* with no prospects of promotion, where the work is often boring and repetitive, or is casual with no proper protection. These sort of jobs may seem quite attractive when you have just left school; they give you money in your pocket and make no real demands on you, but they won't look so appealing when and if you have a family to support.
- *Open ended jobs* are jobs which give you a chance to move forward, either through the training they offer you or through your

own qualities of personality and hard work.

Sean is in a dead end job at the moment. His work as a scaffolder offers no security and he is not receiving any training. Casual labouring means you need to be fit and ready to work in unpleasant conditions. Although this might seem OK when you're sixteen, especially if it means money in your pocket, it doesn't look so attractive as time goes by.

Winston, on the other hand, has acquired a skill (carpentry) even if he has no formal qualifications in it and he should be able to move forward. He can either work for himself (it's quite easy to do – just look at the cards in your local newsagent offering DIY work, carpentry and painting and decoration), or for a reputable local firm. Winston gets a great deal of job satisfaction from his work. He takes pleasure in doing a job well and seeing the end results. Job satisfaction does not figure highly in Sean's life, however.

Susan and Ayesha have both taken steps towards following a career. When we talk about a career we usually mean the sort of work which is prepared for and which is a long term prospect. We talk about the career ladder and see a career as the process of climbing up that ladder. Often to step on to it in the first place you need qualifications such as exam passes or a university degree, but not always. There are rags to riches stories of people who have started life on the shop floor and risen to be managing director.

Susan has chosen a career, medicine, in which for the first few years of her working life she will have to work long hours for lowish pay. But, as she moves up the career ladder in hospital she will earn a considerable salary. She will also be expected to continue studying even when she starts work in order to be up-to-date with developments in medicine.

Ayesha has embarked on a path which will lead to a career as well. She may or may not go to university, but she will have a good chance to work with a large company where she will have plenty of opportunity to be promoted.

Wanting to follow a career usually means staying in full-time education after school leaving age in order to gain the necessary qualifications, but there are also lots of career openings for school leavers with good examination passes, such as bank work or police work and for some young people this is a good way to start a career.

Whether you decide to stay on at school or not can be influenced not just by what work you want to do, but by your personal and social development.

Sean wanted to leave school as quickly as possible. He wanted to become part of the adult male world of pay packets and pubs. Susan needed the security and sense of belonging that she had in the sixth form at school, and Ayesha needed the independence that college gave her. Winston liked the sense of standing on his own two feet as well, but was perfectly happy attending college on his Youth Training scheme.

These young people have all made decisions about which direction they wanted to go in. These decisions will shape their lives but they are not irreversible. If they don't work out they will need to be able to respond flexibly and perhaps take off in another direction altogether.

If Susan fails her 'A' levels and doesn't get into the medical school she can still train as a nurse and enter medicine that way, or get work with a drug company or as a medical technician.

Sean may decide that he wants a steady job with prospects after all and go back to take an access course at college or a government training scheme.

Ayesha may do so well that she can go to university. She could end up doing research or teaching. Winston has the sort of skills and attitudes which will mean that he will never be short of some kind of work.

Of course, even if you make all the 'right' decisions you may still not get a job, but thinking ahead and planning your path increases your chances. It's not too soon to start thinking about these questions in your third year at secondary school; not about precisely what you want to do, but whether you want to stay on or not, whether you fancy college or YTS and so on.

Talk to your parents, your older brothers and sisters, your teachers and find out what they did. Ask them if they would make the same decisions if they had their time again – adults love talking about things like that – and see what you can learn from their experiences *and* their mistakes.

CHOICES

Let's look again at the choices you can make at the end of your fifth year and sum up their pros and cons:

STAYING ON AT SCHOOL

You may want to do this for several reasons:
- because you want to follow an 'A' level course
- because you want to re-sit GCSE exams
- because your school offers a good pre-vocational course – aimed at improving your general education and giving some tasters for work experience.

Some of the advantages of staying on at school are:

- that you feel familiar with the place and know your way around
- that the teachers know you and your strengths and weaknesses
- that you will be with friends whom you know
- that you're treated differently in the sixth form (you're given more freedom, you don't have to wear uniform, you're given free periods, you're allowed off the premises etc)
- that you may like the feeling of being a senior, and being given responsibility, perhaps as a prefect (which, by the way, is something that employers are rather keen on, as it shows you can take responsibility and be trusted)
- that most schools now offer a wide variety of courses in the sixth form, so they are not just interested in the academic kids staying on.

There are disadvantages of course:

- You may still feel that you are being treated too much like a school kid and not enough like a young adult
- You may be fed up with rules and regulations which even sixth formers have to conform to

- You may find that your school does not offer a wide enough range of choices or have the facilities that you need to do what you want
- You may feel that you've had enough of the educational system and want a job.

If you decide not to stay on at school you have three main choices:

- you can go on to some form of college education
- you can take up a youth training scheme
- you can look for a job

GOING TO COLLEGE

There are three main types of college for 16-19 year-olds.

Further Education Colleges

Your parents will probably remember these as technical colleges. Originally they provided courses for young people who wanted to learn a trade, or gain skills in office work. Many young people attended on a day release basis as they already had a job.

Nowadays further education colleges still offer such courses and a wealth of others besides. You can take GCSEs or 'A' levels, BTEC courses, City and Guilds and Royal Society of Arts qualifications, as well as a host of pre-vocational courses, access courses for slightly older people and so on. In fact, they offer a huge variety of choice which can seem very confusing at first. We'll look in more detail at how you go about choosing a college course in the next chapter.

In large cities the colleges often specialise – in London, for example, you have the London College of Fashion, the London College of Printing, Westminster College which specialises in catering, and many more. Students often come from outside London to attend these specialist colleges but most people go to the college nearest home.

The advantages of F.E. college are:
- that you are treated as an autonomous young adult, i.e. you are seen to be responsible for yourself
- that if you haven't been too good at school you can make a new start
- that there is a huge range of courses to choose from
- that most colleges have up-to-date facilities and equipment
- that there are good facilities for recreation

The disadvantages are:
- that F.E. college may seem very large and impersonal
- that the staff won't know you

- that you may wish that you had stayed at school.

Sixth Form College

In some areas individual schools no longer have sixth forms but all the students who stay on go to a sixth form college which caters for all the schools in the area. Sixth form colleges offer both academic and vocational courses. Some of the advantages of sixth form college are:

- that you are still with your friends
- that sixth form colleges are usually smaller than further education colleges
- that you don't have lots of younger children around

Disadvantages might be:

- a sixth form college may not offer the same number of courses as an F.E. college, or have the same facilities
- it may have an academic bias

Tertiary College

In some areas all post 16 provision is in one institution called a Tertiary college. This is intended to cater for all young people who want to continue with some form of education after school leaving age. It may not all be housed in the same building – often it is spread over several sites which may be quite widely separated. The idea is to create the sort of comprehensive where academic and not so academic young people are catered for by the same institution. Tertiary colleges share the advantages and disadvantages of F.E. colleges.

YOUTH TRAINING SCHEMES

If you don't want to stay on at school or go full-time to college, if you can't get a job or can't decide what to do, then YTS may be the answer. This is a training programme run by the government through the Department of Employment Training Agency (formerly the Manpower Services Commission), and is open to all young people from sixteen to eighteen. It aims to provide training in various skills and is usually a mixture of work experience and college attendance. The programmes last for two years and they vary enormously in what they have to offer. These are some of the schemes available in London and the South East:

> horse and stable management
> stonemason
> dental assistant
> sea fishing
> theatre technician

stockbroking
league football

Many firms in your local area will run Youth
Training Schemes and so will many public and
voluntary bodies.

The YTS has had a lot of bad publicity, some
justified (see 'disadvantages' below). It is possible
that in the near future the government will insist
that all young people who do not have a job have
to take part in a scheme.

The advantages of YTS are:

- that you should receive some useful training
- that you earn a weekly payment
- that you can carry on looking for a job
  while you are on a scheme and leave if you
  find one
- that some schemes, especially those run by
  training agencies, offer tasters of different
  jobs
- that the only alternative may be the dole

The disadvantages are:

- that some employers use it as a source
  of cheap labour
- that you do not always get proper protection
  under the health and safety at work laws –
  there have been several cases of young people
  being killed or injured using unprotected or
  unsupervised machinery

- that you are not always given the training that is promised
- that there is no guarantee of either a job or a proper qualification at the end of the scheme.

It's interesting that compared to France and Germany, Britain has a poor record of training young school leavers. More than two thirds of all young people in Britain have no occupational qualifications.

GETTING A JOB

Of course, you may decide that you don't want to take up any of these options but what you want is a job, as soon as possible.

The type of job that you can get will depend on several things – whether you have any GCSEs or other qualifications, what the job prospects in your area are like, how hard you are prepared to look for work and how soon you start applying for jobs. It will also depend on your appearance and personality, the sort of report you have had from school, and whether you have ever been in trouble with the law.

The next chapter deals with how to go about looking for work so let's briefly look at the advantages and disadvantages of starting work at sixteen.

The advantages are:

- that you start to earn money straight away
- you are one step ahead of your friends who stayed at school to retake exams
- if you are lucky you may find a job that offers you day release to study at college or with its own training scheme.

The disadvantages are:

- that the money you earn may seem a lot now, but in an unskilled job it's not likely to increase
- that you may find yourself missing the company of your own age group
- that you may find the job boring and repetitive after the first few days
- that you might find the discipline of the work place much tougher than you bargained for.

So now you are armed with some facts and ideas about what courses of action are open to you when you reach school leaving age.

In the next chapter we'll look at how you embark on them.

HOW DO I START?

If you make the decision to stay on at school or at college, you have put off the evil hour of actually having to find a job for a year or two. If you go on to university and then do post-graduate work you may even put it off for ten years, but most of you will have to face up to it sooner than that! And of course, you usually embark on a particular course of study at tertiary level with some idea of the field you may want to work in, if not the actual job.

If you're really not sure what you want to do and your family circumstances don't mean that you have to go out and earn a living straight away, then it's better to stay on and take some more GCSEs or take a pre-vocational course of some kind. If money would come in handy, do a general YTS as this will keep your options open.

Since the introduction by the Government

of a new Social Security Act in 1988, as a young person under eighteen you will not be entitled to any social security benefits if you are not working. If you haven't got a job and are not at college then you will have to accept a place on a Youth Training Scheme if you wish to receive any state support. Even being homeless will not necessarily entitle you to benefits! The days when you could live on Social Security until you found a job that you liked are now gone.

TWO IMPORTANT THINGS TO REMEMBER:

- You'll be out at work (touch wood) for far longer than you were at school, so don't be in too much of a hurry to leave. Your school days may not be the best days of your life in the way the old cliché suggests, but your working days may not be all that wonderful either. Think what you'll miss about school before you leave, not afterwards!
- You may not be looking for a job for life, but even a few months in a job you really don't like and aren't suited to can seem like hell. It's worth thinking carefully about the various possibilities that are open to you.

We've already considered one major decision – whether to stay on at school or not. In this chapter I want to take you on a guided tour of how to go about applying for university or college, how to get on to a YTS, and how to look for a job and hopefully get one!

Remember to keep in mind all the aspects of *YOU* that we looked at in the last chapter.

UNIVERSITY OR POLYTECHNIC

If you stay on in the sixth form or take some other form of further education you may decide that you want to continue your studies into Higher Education, at university or polytechnic. You might choose the higher education route for a variety of reasons:

- you need a degree in order to qualify for the job you want to do
- you don't know what job you want to do but a degree always helps
- you're really interested in a particular subject and want to carry on studying it for its own sake
- you fancy three years of student life before settling down

When you apply for university or poly you should have an idea of the course you want to follow – study the prospectuses carefully and ask your teachers' advice – some universities have better reputations for certain subjects than others. It's also always worth having a go at Oxford or Cambridge. You may have to do an entrance exam, but they're not as hard as they seem.

When you have read the prospectuses, go and look around – lots of universities have 'visiting' days, and ask your teachers where they went and if they liked it. Remember you don't necessarily have to do the subject that you were best at at school. There are many areas of study at university that don't even figure in most school curriculums – psychology, philosophy, communications studies, American history, biochemistry, astrophysics, medicine, Russian – you get the picture. You can also do degrees in combinations of subjects.

So think:

- What do I need for what I want to be?
- What am I interested in?
- What would I enjoy doing?

If all three add up to the same area of study – fine. If not, go for what you're interested in and enjoy – you might change your ideas of what you want to be.

To go to university you apply through an organisation called University Central Council on Admissions or UCCA for short, stating your subjects and what you want to study and then wait for offers or interviews. For polys you apply through the Polytechnic Central Admissions System (PCAS). Polys often offer a wider variety of courses than universities and have less stringent entry requirements. Don't despair if you're not offered a place before you get your results. If you do well you may still get a place, or you can always reapply with certainty the following year. You can often change the subject you're studying if you find it really isn't for you when you start to go into it. It usually means repeating a year, though, and you do have to have worked well.

You may want to put off going into higher education for a year and take a job, do community work or be an au pair. That's all right. In fact, it can be an advantage. Similarly, when you've got your higher qualification, you may want to do voluntary work overseas where you can use your knowledge working with people in developing countries, before settling down to your career.

The other thing to bear in mind is that it's always possible to do a degree as a mature student. Say you get to the age of twenty-five or thirty, or even forty or fifty, and decide that you would really like to pick up your education again – there are still avenues open to you. You could apply for an Open University course. You can even do these if you're in prison! Or you could join an access course at a Further Education College or Polytechnic, which could lead to a degree course. So remember – if you miss out on higher education first time round, there is a second chance.

COLLEGE

You may live in a part of the country where there is only one college for your area; it may be a Further Education College, a Tertiary College, or a Sixth Form College. On the other hand, if you live in a large city there may be several colleges to choose from.

Whatever the case, you will probably find that the number and types of courses on offer are cast, and read a bit like a coded message:

BTEC, CPVE, RTITB, GCSE, RSA,
NNEB, C&G . . .

Don't be put off – it's quite easy to code break and there are lots of people who can help you.

If you're thinking of going to college and are

fairly sure of the area you want to specialise in – eg motor mechanics, information technology, community and social work – then you need to find out if there is a local college that specialises in that area. If you are in a one college town, then that college will offer most specialist and general areas. Even colleges that specialise offer a whole range of other courses. If you're not sure what you want to do, then you may want to take a general, or pre-vocational course, and then decide.

Pre-vocational courses are fairly new. We talked a bit about what vocation meant in the last chapter, but in terms of college, vocational training means training for a specific skill or area – electrical engineering, word processing, nursery nursing, for example.

Pre-vocational courses do give you an award – the Certificate of Pre-vocational Education (CPVE). They are one year courses which can lead into more job related training. You can usually get onto a CPVE course without GCSEs. (Some schools run CPVE courses in the sixth form for people who want to stay on.) The courses are designed to give you practical work experience in a variety of areas – business, technical, service, production, plus some general education. You can concentrate on one area or try out a mixture. The actual course you follow should be tailored quite closely to what interests *you* and your final certificate is a certificate of achievement, not a pass or fail.

If college is for you, how do you apply?

First you should talk it over with your Careers teacher, form tutor or Careers Officer – they'll be able to give you background information and point you in the right direction. The next step is to send off for the college prospectuses. You can write or ring. These are usually glossy brochures giving you information on the organisation of the college – including social life – and details of all the courses on offer. Most colleges are divided up into departments; for example, Vauxhall College in London has a Business Education Department, Department of General Education, Department of Technical Studies, Department of Building Crafts and a Department of Continuing Education.

Obviously, if you know that you want to take a course in bricklaying, you can just specify that.

It's worth remembering that the colleges want you as much as you want them. The brochures are designed to sell the college to you, after all.

It's also worth remembering that you don't

have to wait until your final year to send off for the brochures, although you will have to be of school leaving age before you can be given a place.

The brochures arrive and you spend some time looking through them, trying to decipher them and talking about what's on offer with your parents and friends. Some of the questions that you should be considering are:

- What course you want to follow
- What qualifications, if any, are required
- What balance of theory and practical work is involved

In its prospectus, Brixton College, London, offers the following advice to students:

How to apply for a course
It is most important that intending students choose a course within their abilities and appropriate to their future careers (if known). Many traditional courses and qualifications are constantly changing and intending students are strongly advised to consult with teaching staff and careers advisers before making their final selection. The college will do everything it can to help students find the right course for them.

- Whether you get any work experience
- Whether the course is full- or part-time
- How long the course lasts
- What qualification you receive
- Whether the course leads on to a higher qualification

Once you've filled in your application form and sent it off (and make sure you do it early – popular courses like nursery nursing get filled up really quickly) then you have to wait. The college will eventually get in touch with you and inform you that:

- you've been accepted for the course that you want
- you must attend for an interview with the course tutor before you can be accepted
- you must attend to take a short college assessment in English and Maths
- there are no vacancies
- you do not qualify for that particular course but they suggest others

If you've applied for more than one course or college and they all accept you then you've got the pleasant job of choosing the one that suits you best.

If you don't get accepted at all, it's worth contacting the colleges in September to see what places they have left. People sometimes don't take up their places and you may be lucky.

Finally, if you are going to college you should find out whether you qualify for a grant, and apply straightaway.

YOUTH TRAINING SCHEMES (YTS)

If you don't want to go to college, but feel that you need some more training and work experience before you decide on the job you want, then you might consider a Youth Training Scheme. Or you might find yourself without a job and having to take part in a YTS because you are not entitled to unemployment benefit.

There is a huge variety of schemes – some run by large companies such as Ford, others by small local firms and others by local councils and the Department of Employment Training Agency. They are open to all sixteen-year- olds and last for two years. You are eligible for YTS until you are eighteen. After that there are other sorts of schemes available.

YTS is what is known as a roll-on, roll-off, programme because you can start it or leave it at any time (within the age limits) and you can re-start it as many times as you want to – or have to! If you lose or leave a job under the age of eighteen you will be expected to 'roll-on' to a scheme.

All schemes should have the following things in common:

- the payment of a weekly allowance
- the payment of travelling expenses over a certain limit
- a period of induction when you learn about the programme
- experience of different types of work
- a chance to do off the job training, usually at college

You should also get:

- an opportunity to gain a vocational qualification or a credit towards one
- a chance to learn about computers and information technology
- a general training in social and life skills

You can apply for a YTS through the Careers Office or Job Centre, or directly to the employer. Sometimes they are advertised in local papers. The Department of Employment Training Agency produces lots of material about the scheme which your Careers Officer will have, and most areas have local training agencies which run programmes and provide information.

When you start a scheme you should receive a Training Agreement which spells out your rights and responsibilities, and those of the training organisation. It's important to know what your entitlement to holidays and sick pay are, also the health and safety procedures and your legal rights.

When the schemes first started they were strongly criticised on these grounds. Young people were badly injured and some even killed because the employers had not taught them the proper safety precautions or had put them to work on dangerous or unguarded machinery or without supervision.

There was also a lot of concern that employers were using trainees as cheap labour, not teaching them anything useful and generally exploiting them. If you are going on to a scheme you should bear this in mind and if you do feel that you are being abused or taken advantage of, you should report it to your Careers Officer and leave the scheme.

You should always join the union that operates in your workplace. We'll look in more detail at this later, but your union representative or shop steward can also help you if you are being badly treated.

If you find difficulty getting on to the sort of scheme you want, then make a fuss. If you are a girl and you want to learn a skill such as electronics or bricklaying, or if you want training in the new technology but find yourself channelled towards office or shop work, make a fuss. If you are a member of an ethnic minority group and find that there are some firms that won't recruit you onto their YTS programmes – make a fuss.

Remember, there's no guarantee of a job at the end of a scheme, although if you are lucky you may be employed by the people you have been doing work experience with. You can apply for jobs at any time during the scheme, and you should be allowed time off for interviews. And of course if you are offered a job, you can leave the scheme. Some young people who are sent on schemes already have jobs, and some employers may demand it of you when they take you on.

Do shop around for the scheme that suits you best because they do vary enormously in what they have to offer.

And do remember – if you think you are getting a raw deal – don't suffer in silence.

LOOKING FOR A JOB

If you decide that you want to start work as soon as you leave school then you need to get organised. You need to think seriously about what you want from work (and life, for that matter) because there aren't many jobs that you can go into at sixteen which have particularly good prospects.

If you get good GCSE results then you've got a better chance, or if you know someone who can give you a start. Some employers offer to train you 'on the job' and there may still be a few apprenticeships available, but generally the sort of job you are likely to get will be a dogsbody job – and you need to be aware of that.

You will be the youngest, least experienced person there – the office junior, the fetcher and carrier, the tea maker – and you will often be given repetitive and plain boring work to do. If you stick it out and show that you can do it well and cheerfully then you may be moved on to more interesting work.

Some jobs – the dead end jobs that we talked about in the last chapter – never get any better. You may find yourself working with a good bunch of people and that can compensate for the boredom of the tasks, but factory work, labouring and service work, especially in catering, tend not to lead anywhere.

Although for a while, having your pay packet in your hand at the end of the week may make it all seem worthwhile, you also need to remember that your wage is unlikely to increase very much.

Another thing to beware of in these sort of jobs is that young people are often sacked when they reach eighteen and the employer has to increase their wages. They then take on another young school leaver in your place. I know quite a few young people to whom this has happened.

So bearing these cautions in mind, let's work our way through the job jungle. Remember that some of this information will apply to you at whatever age and with whatever qualifications you eventually seek work.

JOB ADVERTISEMENTS

The Careers Office

Your local authority Careers Office usually gets sent notice of job vacancies by local firms. If you have a careers interview and you make it clear what you are interested in, then they will notify you if anything suitable turns up. It's also worth checking with them yourself on a regular basis. Lots of Careers Offices produce lists of jobs which they circulate to schools so your Careers teacher should know about them too.

Job Centres

These are found in most local high streets and are run by the Department of Employment. (They used to be called Labour Exchanges.) They have a window full of cards advertising vacancies and inside lots more are displayed under various headings. Many of the jobs advertised are for unskilled or semi-skilled work. Although you can just copy down the details of the job and apply yourself, it's a good idea to talk to the staff who will be able to advise you. The jobs on display change regularly so it's worth visiting daily and applying for all the jobs that appeal to you.

Employment Agencies

Employment agencies are private firms in the business of advertising jobs to make a profit. They usually specialise in a particular area; for example, in London and most large cities there are lots of agencies dealing exclusively with office work. You can see advertisments for these on the tube, in the evening papers, in bus shelters and even on TV. Most of the jobs they have on offer require some form of experience or qualifications, but it could be worth checking them out, particularly if it is office work you are interested in and you have a keyboard or business studies qualification from school. Many such agencies offer temporary work but temporary work can often lead on to a permanent job if you fit in well and work hard.

Newspapers

Jobs at all levels are advertised in newspapers. Many jobs have to be advertised by law so you can open the newspaper and see an advertisement for the managing director of Channel Four, or for a trainee plumber. You should scan the newspapers regularly for job advertisements, whatever your qualifications and experience. The so called 'quality papers' – *The Guardian, The Independent, The Times* and *The Daily Telegraph* carry ads aimed mainly at people with at least 'A' levels and usually degrees or other professional qualifications who are looking for a career, or who are moving up a career ladder. But there are often quite a few jobs advertised with less demanding requirements. The 'popular' press – *The Mirror, The Mail, The Express* etc have advertisements for skilled and semi-skilled jobs, and often for office work and catering. If you live somewhere that has a local paper it's usually a good source of similar jobs. Local papers are probably where you're most likely to find work as a school leaver. Try to get hold of them as soon as they are published though, as there is always a lot of competition.

Trade Magazines

Specialist magazines such as *Farmers Weekly* and *Construction News* also have job ads, but usually ask for specific qualifications. If there is an area you are keen on, though, it's worth having a look through a specialist magazine. You can sometimes find them in the reference section of your local library – they can be expensive to buy.

If you are interested in domestic work or child-care, *The Lady* magazine is full of advertisements for au pairs, home helps and nannies.

Situations Vacant

Sometimes you will see vacancies advertised directly in shop windows 'Assistant Wanted – Apply Within' or on cards in newsagents and such like. Keep your eyes open as you walk around.

A few firms and factories still have vacancy boards outside but these are few and far between. Still, if you have a trading estate near you you could check it out.

Local Radio

Many local radio stations now run job hunt programmes where vacancies are advertised on the air. You can often also get information packs and advice from them. For example, Capital Radio offers a free job finding kit, and also has a job mates service where you are put in touch with someone who can advise you on looking for work.

OTHER WAYS OF FINDING WORK

Family and friends

You may be one of the lucky ones who has a job waiting for you when you leave school thanks to some contact or family connection. Even if you haven't you should ask your family and friends if they know of any jobs going and if they could keep an eye open for you. If they are working already they may know when a vacancy is about to arise and can give you advance warning. They can also often give you good advice based on their own job hunting experiences.

Direct application

Many large firms do not advertise vacancies but that doesn't mean they haven't got any – large stores, fast food chains, banks, the civil service, the post office, the armed services, the police – all recruit directly. Of course they do advertise sometimes, but they tend to be general adverts of the 'Join the Army and See the World' variety. In all the above cases you should write directly to the firm or organisation, or ring up a local branch and ask to speak to the personnel officer.

Giz a Job

You can try the direct approach anywhere – just walk in and ask. You've got nothing to lose and you may have a lot to gain. You need to be fairly confident though and good at selling yourself. (Look back to Chapter Two and remind yourself of how to build up your self image.)

You can also advertise yourself – in a local paper, in the newsagent's window, – but beware of being too general – 'willing worker, anything considered' or 'young girl offers cleaning services' could lead you into trouble. There are people, fortunately not very many, who exploit and take advantage of young people sexually and who may respond to such advertisements. Don't put your phone number on them – it could lead to upsetting and unpleasant calls, and do get your parents or some other responsible adult to check out the genuineness of anyone who answers your ad.

Setting up in Business

You can also set up your own business, either on your own, or with friends. You can set yourselves up as:

gardeners
child-minders
painters and decorators

delivery services
removals
cleaners

window cleaners	dog walkers
typing services	shoppers . . .
odd job people	

I'm sure you can think of more ideas. There may be government grants available to help you. Your local job centre will be able to advise you on this.

Casual and seasonal work

In some parts of the country you can often find seasonal and casual work. In farming areas help is needed at crop picking time – pulling potatoes, picking strawberries etc – while at the seaside and in other tourist spots the summer season generates extra jobs – selling ice cream, deck chair attendants, work in hotels and restaurants.

It's probably not worth leaving home for this sort of work unless accommodation is provided. The cost of finding somewhere to live in a seaside town might take care of your earnings.

If you are a bit older and adventurous you can look for casual work abroad – grape picking in France for example, or helping at summer camps in America. Your local reference library will have a directory of jobs like these, so will most large book shops.

OUT OF WORK

If after all your efforts you still fail to get a job, or if you lose the job you have, one way of filling in your time usefully is to do voluntary work. There's an enormous range of such work available, from helping in hospitals, teaching adult literacy, helping old people or mentally handicapped children, to working on local conservation projects and archaeological digs. You can get information from your local reference library or contact Community Service Volunteers. Your local town hall or social services may know of other projects that welcome volunteers.

It's a good idea to join your local youth club too. They have a whole range of leisure activities on offer and it also means that you can socialise with other young people, many of whom will be in the same boat.

Local Adult Education Institutes run day and evening classes that you can join at reduced rates if you are out of work. They provide a wealth of courses from general interest and hobby-type courses through help with literacy and numeracy to specific skills such as car maintenance and book binding. You can also study foreign languages or more conventional 'academic' subjects.

It can be demoralising to be out of work but

don't sit at home cut off from human contact and new ideas.

APPLYING FOR A JOB

So now we've looked at some of the ins and outs and ups and downs of the job market, how do you actually go about applying for one?

There are plenty of books and leaflets available that give you good advice on how to apply for jobs, so all I'll give you here is a brief run down on it. You've probably spent time at school practising writing letters of application, filling in application forms and writing out your curriculum vitae.

Action Plan

In advance
Make sure that you have written a personal description or Curriculum Vitae (CV) and made copies of it. It can be hand-written or typed.

The advertisement
Read it carefully, check that you have what it is asking for; list for yourself the reasons you would like the job and why you think you can do it.

The application

Depending on what the advertisement asks you to do,

EITHER

ring, say who you are, who you want to speak to about what and why. (Don't get cut off; do have a pencil and paper handy.)

OR

write, asking for an application form. (Fill it in carefully, neatly and honestly.)

OR

write a direct letter of application including your personal details and CV, your reason for wanting the job and for thinking you can do it.

The Interview

- Prepare for it. It is a good idea to get your family or friends to give you a mock interview
- Make a list of all the things you want to say about yourself
- Get there with a bit of time to spare
- Look clean and neat
- Be polite but confident
- Smile (but not too much!)
- Try not to give single word answers to questions
- Make sure that you show that you actually

want the job. Don't be off-hand
- Ask them questions, about conditions, holidays, training and promotion
- Remember to say goodbye and thank you

You can, and should, apply for as many jobs as possible that interest you and that you think you can do. Don't be down hearted if you don't get the first one that you try for – very few of us do. As you keep trying, your interview technique will improve and you will have more idea what to expect. Interviews are always a bit of an ordeal whatever age you are, and sweaty palms and butterflies in the stomach are quite natural.

Most of this advice applies to you if you are applying for work at sixteen, eighteen, or after leaving university or college.

You may have one job for life or a succession of jobs. You may start off doing one thing and end up as something completely different. In the next chapter we'll look at the job histories of some people who have followed a variety of paths through the job jungle.

WORKING LIVES: FOUR CASE HISTORIES

What we've discussed so far may seem a bit theoretical to you, but if we look at some examples of real working lives, it's easier to see what the decisions and choices we've been talking about mean in practice.

In this chapter four people – a freelance television director, a nursery teacher, a police constable and a Careers Officer – talk about what influenced their choice of career and what helped to shape them. They describe their school days, the choices and decisions they made, their ups and downs. Some of them found what they wanted to do by accident, others had a fairly clear idea all along. Some went through lots of changes, with lots of false starts, others had a relatively troublefree time.

What they all have in common is that they have had to deal with all the aspects of themselves

– their ambitions, their strengths and weaknesses. This is what you will have to do too on your own unique path to the future. So let's see what they've got to say.

MARILYN GAUNT – FREELANCE TELEVISION DIRECTOR

I went to a mixed junior school – I loved it. I enjoyed playing, I was a bit of a tomboy, I liked messing about and I didn't pass my 11 plus. So in 1958 I went to an all girls secondary modern school in Leeds. I was in the A stream and after the first year exams I found myself fifth in the class without trying. I'd experienced what it was like to be down at the bottom in primary school so I thought that with a bit more effort I could be top. That started my competitive spirit and I became a real swot, although I still enjoyed acting the goat. I came second in the next lot of exams, then I came top and from then on I was top of the class.

So the best thing that happened to me was failing the 11 plus. The ability to do things by my own efforts became very important to me as a result.

The next stage was when I was thirteen. I did a 13 plus examination for late developers but didn't do quite well enough to transfer to grammar school so I stayed on in the GCE stream where the largest class was only twenty and a lot of the teachers were really keen on helping girls achieve. It was very arts oriented – the only science that we did was Biology. I loathed Maths. I was terrible at it so in the third year when we could choose between Maths and Art I dropped it. Art was my favourite subject; I'd always wanted to be a painter.

I took seven 'O' levels. I loved school. I was a prefect and all that. I loved Art and English and History, especially Social History – all about people and what makes us what we are – which I suppose is why I'm now doing social documentaries.

We did have careers advice. I was still a bit of a tomboy, always fantasizing adventures and wanting to do things that were different so I told the Careers Officer that I'd like to be an RAC lady riding around on a scooter or I'd like to join the army and go all over the world, but she said I'd just end up in Catterick (a big army camp in Yorkshire) and that would be the end of me. I was easily dissuaded so I went to art college instead.

I'd been going to Saturday morning art classes at Leeds Art College since I was fourteen just to do extra art because I enjoyed it, so I applied there and got in at sixteen. I did five years there. I got a scholarship when I was eighteen but before that I had to do a Saturday morning job to pay for paints and materials. Abstract art was all the rage then and I got side-tracked into it. I wasn't very good at it and so I only ended up with an average sort of pass which was OK if you wanted to teach. It looked as if it was the only option open to me.

However, in the first year we had made a short 8mm film in a small group and I'd really enjoyed it, especially the experience of working with other people and working out ideas together. So as well as applying to Goldsmiths College in London to do an Art Teacher's diploma I also applied to the Royal College of Art, which was the only place that had a film and TV school to study film. To everybody's surprise I was accepted. I was lucky to get a grant though, as I couldn't have gone otherwise. Although I'd gone to the movies as a kid I'd never had a great passion for them, other than adventure films, but once I started the course I found I could actually make decisions which I knew were right – especially in editing films – and that gave me a great deal of confidence.

I made a short film about a tramp on a bus. I hired a bus for the day from Leeds corporation, got my mother to play the conductress, a mate of my boyfriend's to play the tramp and roped in other friends and relations to help. My main college film was a half hour documentary about Leeds Youth Theatre Workshop and the work they did with a great cross section of kids.

While I was at the RCA I was given a chance to work as assistant editor on a BBC series in term time. It was unpaid but it was marvellous experience. I learnt an enormous amount about practicalities and decided that I would like to be an editor as I got a great deal of satisfaction from it.

I left the RCA in 1970 with an MA, a silver medal and my documentary film. I applied to the BBC but they didn't want me – they only wanted Oxbridge graduates at the time. I was getting nowhere fast when a friend suggested I show my film to some people at Yorkshire TV. They weren't interested in the film, but two weeks later I got a letter from the head of film offering me a job as a trainee cutting room assistant, which was pretty much the bottom rung of the ladder.

The problem in those days was that if you didn't have a union ticket you couldn't get a job, and if you didn't have a job you couldn't get a union ticket. It's changing a bit now.

That was the beginning of an eight year period where I didn't do any directing. I served an apprenticeship really, though a lot of it was drifting. I was a year at Yorkshire doing assistant editing; it was quite a servile job, picking up trimmings and logging shots. It's got to be done of course and it's part of the long haul to getting to be an editor.

Still, I got my union ticket and was also making little films with the drama workshop which was now called Interplay. They were planning to make a longer film about their summer project and were hoping to borrow equipment from a BBC cameraman that someone knew. He was a contract freelance cameraman for *Nationwide* which was a current affairs magazine programme and he needed a sound recordist, so he suggested that we made the film for Interplay together, with me doing the sound recording. If we got on well together, I could go freelance as his sound recordist for *Nationwide*.

I actually enjoyed it very much. The sound equipment was very heavy and I had a huge bruise on my hip from carrying it around. One of the reasons why women weren't supposed to do sound recording was that the equipment was considered to be too heavy for them. But I managed. In fact a baby in one arm and a bag full of shopping in the other's a lot heavier! When I finally took the sound recordist job I got a big piece of foam and stuck it down my trousers!

Then started two-and-a-half years of working

on the road, on location, which I enjoyed for the first year. We worked all over Britain and abroad sometimes, staying in posh hotels. Sound recording is very skilled work; you are monitoring levels of sound, checking for distortion, listening all the time, but you're also observing what the cameraman's doing and watching the programme come together.

The first film I recorded was a walk along the Pennine Way. I had to use radio mikes which I'd practised wiring up to my parents, and then drew diagrams of what to do which I hid up my sleeve so that the director wouldn't realise I'd never done it before. I'd not had any training, except what the cameraman had given me. He'd also taught me how to solder and repair equipment. After two years he got a job as a director and as I didn't get on with his successor I packed it in. I also realised that I wasn't going to get to direct that way.

I spent a short time on the dole then screwed myself up to go back to Yorkshire TV as an assistant editor. I was really a general dogsbody doing all sorts of odds and ends for them, but I did get to do some research as well, until I was told that someone else was coming in to do that job. I was out on a limb again.

Then I saw an advertisement for a researcher on *This is Your Life*. It wasn't a programme which I enjoyed watching but it was based in London and I thought I'd apply for it. I had an interview, got the job and moved back south. It wasn't part of a great career plan but I needed production experience. I'd got the technical experience, editing, sound recording etc – and I'd also done some directing. But the production side is the most common route to directing, often through being a researcher. Production Assistants have much less chance because what they do is still seen very much as women's work, not as a proper career, even though they often have a great deal of experience. It's still seen as a glorified secretarial job.

I really enjoyed working on *This is Your Life*. The producer was a very nice man who believed that you had to get people to trust you enough to tell you bad as well as good things and know that you wouldn't abuse their trust. I learnt to communicate and talk to people and put them at their ease. It was a great educational experience for me. There was also the detective work of trying to find Jock from Stirling who'd been in the army in 1945 and so on. It was very satisfying.

I did it for three years, but I also did some more sound recording during that time. Even in 1977 I was still the only woman sound recordist in the country who had a union ticket and I was asked to be part of an all-woman crew making a film about the traditional way of life of women in Morocco for a series called *Disappearing World*. It was also the first film by the only woman camera operator at the time. We also had a woman director and a woman anthropologist. We were the first all-woman crew ever to be employed by a Network Company and we felt that it was really important that we shouldn't be just as good as a male crew, we should be better. We just couldn't afford to fail because that would have messed it up for the next generation. If a woman fails it's seen to be because she's a woman, but if a man fails it's just seen as something to do with a difficult task. I can't stand it when I see women doing a job sloppily because they are judged by it more than men. We've got to be better if we want to be accepted.

I've never come across any intentional chauvinism. I may have been lucky, and I think that a lot of men are just as much victims of their upbringing as women. I've never felt that being a woman has stopped me doing what I wanted to do but I have had the burden of having to prove myself all the time – to prove that I could do it – whereas men don't often have that.

In the third season of *This is Your Life* Thames TV advertised three vacancies for trainee directors and I got one of these. I then started directing properly, in the studio as well as on film. I was the only woman, I was also the oldest person in the team, but I'd got a lot of experience. I think I had the respect of the film crews because I knew about the technical side and I understood a lot of the problems – the cutting room is the best way to learn to be a director – you see all the mistakes!

I did nine months' basic training and was then given a two year contract with the company. I did *Magpie*, and live studio work which I loved. It was a great high and gave you instant feedback. I also directed some schools programmes but I really wanted to get back to documentary film making. And this is where you can never plan your life completely.

I'd kept in touch with the anthropologist I'd worked with in Morocco and she asked me if I would direct a series of films she wanted to make on the life of women in the Middle East. It was a really difficult project, making films in a language you don't understand, doing everything through an interpreter, but it was very challenging. I did one film in Lebanon (we were going to do two, but the civil war intervened) and two in Egypt about women and political, economic and religious change.

I went back to Thames after that and made two films for them; one about a girl having plastic surgery because she'd been terribly burnt, and one about a reunion of my class from secondary school. They were my first two network documentaries. Social documentaries became my specialism really. I'm interested in people and what makes them tick and all the little details of life which to me are just as important as the big issues. I like it when so-called ordinary people make profound statements; it's like people giving you a gift.

Lately I've done a lot of documentaries about people's lives. I mainly work on a series for Yorkshire TV called *First Tuesday*, but I have my own production company.

Women have always been an important influence in my life – my grandmother, who looked after me a lot, and my mother, who worked as a weaver. She always said, 'We've got nothing to leave you except your education'. I always wanted to do well for her sake.

ANDREW LYNCH – NURSERY TEACHER

I went to a co-educational boarding school which was based on a charitable foundation. My mother was in the drapery trade and so my brothers and I had our fees paid for us.

I went there when I was six and stayed straight through into the lower sixth. The school had streams based on whether you did Latin (which meant you went to university), Economics (which meant you would go into banking or trade) or Social Studies. You were firmly put in your place if you were doing Social Studies, because it was only a CSE. I was put in that stream.

I always felt that I was given a very bad deal on it. I don't think I was the sort of person who was easy to educate – too badly behaved I expect and not particularly good academically. I always got into trouble. I must have been a pain to any teacher that I had and I know there are a lot of teachers there who were utterly amazed that a) I decided to become a teacher and b) that I managed to succeed and that I'm still doing it. I think certainly if I'd been given any careers advice at school it would have been 'don't bother!'

There was a whole group of people in my stream who were given the label 'non-attainers'. It's peculiar, because I met a few of them later on and a lot of them had actually got to university and proved a lot of people wrong. I think it's dreadful when you're given the label of being bottom stream.

I certainly didn't get terribly good grades, just the minimum to scrape into Teacher Training

College. As to advice when I was at school – I was always reasonably good at Art, and enjoyed the creative side of things like Drama. I'd always liked the idea of doing something along those lines. Now if you're good at Art, people will generally say, 'Don't bother. You've got to be brilliant to do Art.' I got very close to the Art teacher, who was a crusty old colonel type who ran the cadet force. He encouraged me when I expressed the idea that I wanted to do Art. Most of the other teachers were quite anti, but this one said, 'Give it a try.'

I left school a year early. I wasn't getting anything out of it any more. It's a very womb-like experience, a private school like that where you've been for more than ten years. This meant I had a period before I went to college and I didn't particularly want to stay at home because my mother would have made my life hell and found me some silly job to do and I wanted to do something interesting. I was interested in those glamorous things abroad, like Voluntary Service Overseas, but they wouldn't take me because I was only sixteen.

At that time they had, and I think it still exists, something called Community Service Volunteers which is an organisation which places people in hospitals, play schemes etc. It appealed to me because it was a chance to get away from home so I was interviewed and sent as a volunteer to a mental hospital just outside Dumfries in Scotland.

It was actually quite peculiar. It sounds as if it was a big move, but funnily enough, after coming from a private boarding school, it wasn't very different. The hospital was completely self-sufficient, like a little town with a farm and factories. I did voluntary work there attached to the community centre. It involved taking films round the wards. I did some Art therapy classes and was generally involved in running the social side of things and making friends with some of the younger patients who needed that attention.

I was applying for college places while I was there. I applied to Goldsmiths College which is a good one for Art teachers, but I couldn't get to the interview and they sent my papers on to my second choice. I went for an interview there and they offered me a place but as they had no vacancies left in secondary education they asked if I'd mind taking a place in junior education. Well, by that time it was so late and I was so relieved to be accepted that I said I'd do it. It seems as if the decisions made when I was starting off my college career were not exactly a series of mistakes, but things that happened to me which I thought I might as well give a go.

I enjoyed and wasted my time at college. I often wonder how effective it is letting people go straight from school to college then back to school again. Even though I'd done ten months at the hospital which looked good on paper and was good experience, it wasn't really the outside world.

I left college in 1975 and after applying for jobs in lots of Education Authorities I got taken on by Inner London.

I was put in a mixed junior school as a fourth year teacher. I was working in a team which was a good way to start a probationer. I did six years there. It was a very typical way for a man to start. You were given the older children. I would have been horrified if they had given me first years. None of my experience covered that. It was expected that if you were a man you would be given the older children. I was given a special post for boys' games so I had to take out the football team and train them. You had to go round yelling at children because as a man you were expected to be a disciplinarian. So I fell into that sort of role. I had a science post as well – another man's subject!

Anyway, after six years I was getting very stale and also very uptight because going round being a football playing shouter isn't very good for anyone. I was actually considering getting out altogether because I really wan't enjoying it.

I volunteered to be moved to another school

and the one they sent me to had an infant school as well. The Head was very into Drama and Theatre so I was given the opportunity to develop in different ways. They already had a man doing football there, so I didn't have to do that. I was able to do what I really wanted.

It was good there was an infant department because over the years I'd got more and more interested in teaching young children. I found that I liked working with them and I found that I was changing as a person. It took a long time but I found I was less stressed and happier with myself. I started taking younger children – the Head had given me a first year class. I enjoyed teaching them very much but was honestly not sure about how well I was performing. It was a longish time since I'd been to college and there had been a lot of changes in educational thought and practice since then. I'd had some infants in my first year and I'd enjoyed teaching them so I asked the Head if I could have an entirely infant class. This caused a bit of comment because men and infants don't usually go together. But I was actually being able to be what I wanted to be. I didn't have to do football any more if I didn't want to. I didn't have to yell at children. Suddenly it was a positive thing being a man, not a negative one. The children were looking to me as a man because they liked me. Most children don't come across men caring for them; women are the people who are constantly with them as mothers or teachers.

A lot of the children didn't have fathers, so there was an emotional gap I was able to fill. And what I found peculiar was that somewhere in *me* there was an emotional gap that *they* filled. Recognising that was a useful thing. I worked there for six years and then asked if I could go on a course that would teach me more about infant teaching. I knew a man who was a nursery teacher but I wasn't really sure whether I wanted to do that because in teaching the younger the people you teach, the less important you are considered. Still, I got a term's secondment to do an Early Year's course, which was basically re-training as a nursery teacher. The course included two terms based in a nursery, which is where I work now.

It's been a great experience. Now that I'm doing it I can't see myself going back to teach juniors again.

Nursery tends to be the first experience children get of school. They come here at three-and-a-half. I like it because they need you. You are in control of their learning. You don't sit and tell them things, you provide them with experiences and a framework for them to do their own learning. I like the idea of getting away from the role of being a teacher. You can't hide behind it with nursery kids. I'm called by my first name. You have to get the kids with you because they want to be, not because you're a teacher. You're just another adult to them so you can just be yourself. I'm rather proud of being a man in the nursery. I like to say to people, 'I'm in the nursery.' It's different. You're valued and you get positive feedback. It's nice to be able to provide a stable male role-model for lots of children who don't have it at home.

It's also nice working with Gloria, the nursery nurse, being a black person. I think we make a nice minority team!

I think it's breaking the mould. I'm relaxed with young children and I like it, I don't have to work with others' preconceived notions. I think it's good for men generally. I think there are a lot of men like me, perhaps with a slightly sensitive nature, who aren't allowed to admit to that side of their nature in the work that they do.

DORIS YIADOM – POLICE CONSTABLE

I didn't always want to be in the police force. I think the idea first came to me when I was about nine, but then I was put off by the Brixton riots.

What I really wanted to be was a commercial pilot – but I didn't have the brains. I was told that you needed three 'A' levels – English, Maths and Physics – and I couldn't get those, so I thought I'd go for air traffic control and get through in that way. But I went for an interview and didn't get in. They said there was another way round it – I could pay for a commercial course in flying, but that would have cost thousands of pounds so *that* was out of the question.

I'd been to loads of different primary schools and then to Mayfield Girls Secondary School. I took some CSEs and also English 'O' level which I passed, then I went to college and passed three more 'O' levels. I think I got fed up with the studying after I took two 'A' levels, Maths and Law, and failed Maths. I thought 'What can I do with only one 'A' level?' While I was at college I applied to go to university to do Physical Education – Sports Science and Management. There are only five universities in the country that do it, and I got turned down by all five! I could have gone to a Higher Education college to do it but I'd had enough of studying.

I applied to join the police in 1986, about nine months after leaving college. I was working nights in Sainsbury's and wondering what other job I could be doing. I was going round the Job Centres looking for something interesting because I didn't want just anything. I would stick at things for a certain time knowing I could leave in the end but I didn't know what to do in the long term.

One day I was looking at the cards in the Job Centre and they were advertising for prison officers and police constables. I asked about both of them. You had to be twenty-one to be a prison officer but you could apply to the police at eighteen. I went down to Victoria to the recruitment centre and decided to apply. They showed you films that made it look very attractive. There are so many stories in the media about what the police are like and I thought 'Well, I can either go in and try it for myself, or believe the stories'. It's not half as bad as I thought it would be from that point of view, but the work itself is a lot harder than I'd imagined. It's stressful, there's a lot of pressure on you in the first two years.

I went in in June 1987 and finished at training school in October. Then I was posted to this station where I've been since. You spend about five months at the college at Hendon. There are about 700 people there at a time and you have an intake every five weeks. We had one of the largest intakes of women because they are beginning to take more women on. In our class we had seven girls and sixteen lads but in one class it was equal, ten of each. This was unheard of because before it had usually been about three women in a class of twenty-five. They're calling out for women now. It's a lot easier to get into the job if you are a woman but once you're in it's actually very male oriented.

It's very chauvinist; it's, 'You make the tea. You deal with the distressed kids and distressed females.' It's a very wide-spread attitude. There are a lot of things that women can't do and even if they can, the men don't like them to – like riots and disturbances for instance. I would tend to hold back myself and let the men go in first because if they go into a riot and there's a woman there on the front line it's a hindrance because they feel they've got to look out for her as well as themselves. So I'm happy to stay out of the way – I'm a coward anyway!

No-one in my family had ever been in the police force. When I went and did it instead of just talking about it they were quite surprised. Mum didn't want me to do it; my Dad didn't either, but he wasn't going to stop me. He's come round now and so has my Mum since she's met some of my colleagues. She'd formed all her ideas from the media. She thought that there would be a lot of racism in the police and that I would find that difficult. I haven't found any, personally, not within the station. There are a lot of jokes, but they're just jokes. If you haven't got a sense of humour anyway you won't survive. I haven't had any problems on the street either; I think that the combination of being black and a woman makes them pay more attention.

As far as the community goes, it's not so much the white as the black community which can be a problem. I've been called 'traitor' a couple of times by kids. They always say it after I've walked past. I take the attitude that if they can't say it in front of me then it's not worth taking up. But I haven't had any violence or anything like that.

You work with the same people on a relief or shift which contains about twenty-five constables. You have to spend two years on relief. One as a trainee and you go two days a month to a training centre. I'm still a probationer because I haven't finished yet.

When you finish you can choose what you want to do. I always thought community policing would be a good thing, being a home beat officer. I think I'd like to do that for the social aspect – talking to people, getting to know members of the public and helping them out.

The thing that I don't like doing at the moment is stopping vehicles and pulling people up for motoring offences. But it's a job. I like it generally. There are things I'm not keen on doing, but you've got to do them anyway. You've got to write your quota of reports and write up processing books about motoring offences.

What I'd really like to do is join the underwater search team when I've finished my probation but you've got to have three or four years' service in before you can specialise. I think I'm attracted to it because they haven't got any women in the team.

Breaking new frontiers can be quite dangerous though, because if you're not accepted they can make life hell for you. I know there are fire women who have a horrible time. It's not like that in the police force although as a probationer they do play jokes on me.

It's not too hard work, but there's a lot to do and a lot to take in. As far as promotion is concerned I'm not sure I would be able to handle that amount of responsibility. After my probation I might start thinking about it but you can't take the sergeant's exam until you've had five years' service and got some experience on the street.

TERRY MILES – INNER LONDON CAREERS OFFICER

I grew up on a new council estate in Mitcham, Surrey. All the other kids went to the local primary school, but my mum sent me to a little private preparatory school which cost £12 a term – that was a lot of money in those days!

The problem was that it was quite a small school and they didn't let you fight in the playground so I wasn't used to being hit at all. The work was very repetitive and the school was quite authoritarian – it just crammed people for exams – it was the 11 plus in those days. I thought at school I was quite thick because I couldn't do a lot of what the other kids could do, but somehow I got through the 11 plus and went to Mitcham Grammar, which was the first 'ordinary' school I'd been to.

I thought it was huge, but by today's standards it was very small – only about 600 kids in all. I started to get bullied in the first year and that went on until about the third or fourth year. It was pretty bad. I used to hide in the toilets and I took up trombone lessons to escape. Everyone in the class used to belt me until one day in the third year I lost my temper and belted someone back. The school never noticed any of this – they just thought I was a lazy little so-and-so.

I fell more and more behind. I'd no idea what was going on in Maths at all – I've still got a mental block about it. I liked English. I liked reading and enjoyed English Literature. I would have enjoyed music if my peer group had allowed me to. I'd never heard of classical music in my life, but in the first year Mr Chapman the music teacher played Holst's *Planets Suite* and I thought it was amazing. But my mates were more into the Beatles and just made fun of me.

I liked Geography and Art but had to choose between them in the second year and chose Geography. I didn't get on with Woodwork at all and I wasn't much good at sports or games. I went through life believing what I'd read in comics – that people who were thick at academic things were automatically good at sports but it wasn't true. Kids that are really smart are good at both.

I hated school but I stayed on into the sixth form to repeat some 'O' levels – I'd only managed to get English Language and Literature and Geography. I looked through the careers literature and thought, 'What can three 'O' levels buy?' They couldn't really buy anything. So I decided I'd stay on. I took Maths and History, but by this time I'd got involved in writing and producing the school magazine. I'd started off writing poems in school detention, because I'd forgotten my other work and the teacher read them and said they were really good. It was amazing – I'd found something I could actually do. I started reading the Liverpool poets and others.

I had friends by this time who were doing Art so I used to go into the Art room and mess around painting pictures. I found out that the school had entered me for the Art exam which I passed – but I failed Maths and History! So I ended up with four 'O' levels and fell between two stools. I was theoretically too clever for an apprenticeship, and anyway I hadn't got Maths and I was too thick to work in a bank or somewhere like that, because I hadn't got five 'O' levels.

I looked through the careers book and the only thing I could find which only wanted four, including Art, was the Ordnance Survey. I wrote off to them and was offered an interview. They said I'd got to bring samples of my art work. I hadn't got any so I borrowed someone else's, took them along with me, and got offered the job! Unfortunately it meant moving to Southampton and as I was only seventeen and had no chance of getting anywhere to live there I didn't go.

So I went along to see the careers officer and she suggested a job in a print metal works as a trainee manager which I got. It was a serious traineeship – they sent me to college once a week to do RSA courses in Commerce and Business Studies but I found it really boring. I also didn't much like the work I had to do the rest of the time – sending orders of metal out to printers. I needed more money too – some friends and I were planning to go to India – so I left and applied to join the fire brigade.

While I was waiting to hear from them I got a job in a cemetery, gardening and looking after graves.

I was accepted by the brigade and was the youngest person there – only eighteen – but I was in for all the wrong reasons. I really only wanted to make money. I bluffed my way through the training. I wasn't very good at tying knots. For some reason on the last day of training they tied me up and left me hanging from the blackboard – and I'd thought that I was one of the lads! Then I was posted to my station. They put you through a lot of initiation ceremonies to find out how tough you are. They usually involve you getting soaking wet. They can be quite cruel and humiliating, but they have to be sure that you can cope and that they can rely on you as part of the team. All the new recruits got it. I was never really accepted because I wasn't aggressive enough. I wasn't any good at volley ball, which they played a lot to strengthen their hands and I wasn't really part of the team. So, although I passed the written exams at the end of my probationary period, I didn't really come up to the mark on the physical 'macho' side and I wasn't taken on. I'd enjoyed quite a lot of it though.

I left and got a job in a toy shop and found that I was quite good at selling things to people. I moved on from there to a job in an Oxford Street shoe shop where I became assistant manager and perfected my sales technique. Never give the customer a chance to say no! I did quite well but didn't get on with one of the manageresses who was too much like a head mistress, so I left.

My next job was in a garage selling petrol. I was the best petrol salesman they'd ever had but eventually I decided I wanted a white collar job again.

I got a nice job as a marketing assistant designing instruction leaflets for a firm selling specialised thermometers which I really enjoyed but the money was awful and I needed money because I was getting married.

We moved to Brighton and I got a job in the K Shoe Shop. I did really well again but money was still a problem. The father of one of the girls who worked there was in charge of British Rail signals and telecommunications in Brighton and I managed to get a job with him.

The job involved taking down all the telegraph poles and wire along the track between Brighton and Littlehampton and replacing it with modern cables. We'd sign on at 7.30, have a cup of tea, get a train to wherever we were working, cut the wire down and coil it up. We'd work quite hard until lunchtime then spend the afternoon drinking tea and playing cards. I was doing so well cutting down wire that they put me on another more specialised gang working on the signals which can be quite dangerous at times.

Then we moved to North Wales. I'd read *The Hobbit* and got really romantic about the countryside, so I applied for a transfer. It was difficult because the rest of the gang spoke Welsh. They expected me to act like a stereotype cockney so I did. Then I got into trouble for lending a friend of mine my privilege ticket for free travel and I had to leave in rather a hurry.

Next I drove a lorry for Corona, delivering fizzy pop to houses in North Wales. I'd only just learnt to drive and on my first day out I ripped the side off the lorry. I really hated that job so that when I saw a job going in the Job Centre for a chainman in a survey team I went and did that. I loved it – it was great – bombing round mapping bits of North Wales for geological surveys, finding out how deep rivers were, tearing round the lanes in a white survey truck. It was fun.

Then they sent me up to Scotland to work

on surveying for the A9 road. I never realised Scotland was so big. My wife didn't like me being away for such long periods of time and I didn't get on with my boss so I went back to Wales. They said I'd been a good worker so they gave me a job in the labs analysing rock samples and mounting them in plastic so they could be examined by electron miscroscopes. I was working alongside geologists and people who'd been to university doing the same sort of work and they asked me why I didn't apply to go to university myself. I'd only got four 'O' levels and knew I didn't qualify but I saw an advertisement in a Sunday paper inviting applications from mature unqualified people so I wrote off, filled in the forms and to my great surprise was given an interview and an offer of a place.

While I was in Wales I'd got involved with Friends of the Earth and quite enjoyed it. I went along to the local Trades Council as a representative and began to take a real interest in local political and environmental issues as well as in politics generally. So I chose to do politics at university in the school of African and Asian Studies.

I got very involved in the politics of the Students Union while I was there and spent a lot of time organising meetings and so on but finally I got disillusioned with what was going on.

Anyway, I eventually got my degree and left university only to become a garage manager again!

But to bring the story up to date I'm now a careers officer for the Inner London Education Authority. I think the fact that I've had so many different jobs myself helps me to help young people.

YOUR RIGHTS AND RESPONSIBILITIES AT WORK

By now you should have enough information to start making some choices about the sort of work you want to do and how you want to go about doing it.

Whatever you end up doing there are certain things which you need to know about to ensure that you're not exploited, discriminated against, taken advantage of, abused, ripped off and generally badly done by. These things are to do with your rights at work. Not many people realise that one of the basic rights in the United Nations Charter of Human Rights is the right to work. Not only should you have the right *to* work you should have rights *at* work. Both these rights have been struggled for and sometimes died for, and even today there are millions who are denied them – not least the millions of unemployed in Britain. So it's important to know about them and to take them seriously.

TRADE UNIONS

The main organisations that defend your right to work and your rights at work are the Trade Unions. All workers (except the police and the armed forces) have the legal right to belong to a trade union. But there are many areas of employment, such as the catering industry, which rely heavily on casual labour, which are very un-unionised and there are also jobs where you may still be sacked for joining a union.

Trades Unions come in for a lot of criticism in the media – that's what the term 'union bashing' means. But working people have fought long and hard in Britain, and are still doing so, to ensure that unions can exist, and can continue.

Until 1871 it was illegal to belong to a union. Only forty years before that, six men, who became known as 'The Tolpuddle Martyrs', were transported to Australia. Their crime was 'unlawfully administering an oath'. In fact, what they had done was to form together to resist a wage cut from eight shillings (forty pence) per week to six shillings (thirty pence) per week, forced on them by the Dorset landowner for whom they worked. Their plight and the cruelty of their sentence so affected public opinion that they were eventually pardoned and returned to England.

The story of the Tolpuddle Martyrs is only one of the many moving examples of working people's struggles to gain a fair wage and decent working conditions – from the matchgirls' strike in 1888 to the seamen's strike in 1988.

So what have we got to show for it? Over nine million people, out of a working population (employed and unemployed) of twenty-seven million are members of eighty-eight trade unions. These fall into four main categories:

- Craft Unions – the oldest form of union, based on proper apprenticeship to a trade
- General Unions – catering mainly for semi-skilled workers such as the Transport and General Workers Union
- Industrial Unions – which represent all workers in a particular industry such as the National Union of Miners
- Non-manual Unions – the most recently formed and the most rapidly expanding unions such as the National and Local Government Officers Association (you can see why it's usually called NALGO for short!) These unions cater mainly for white collar workers.

Some unions are only open to workers in

a particular industry but others have a general membership. When you start your job find out which union most people at your place of work belong to and think about whether to join it too. Why should you? Surely all those old battles are over and done with and your employer will look after you – the law says they should! Well yes, BUT

> – your wages may be low – often as much as 10% less than in a firm which is unionised
>
> – you may not get overtime or proper holiday entitlements
>
> – your working conditions may be bad (machinery unsafe, toilets filthy, office overcrowded . . .)
>
> – you may get the sack

If you don't belong to a union it's much harder to insist on your rights. If you have to go to law to do so it can be expensive, time consuming and you can still be out of a job at the end of the day. Here's what the union can offer:

> 1. It can ensure that you get your legal rights – protection against unfair dismissal, sex and race discrimination; equal pay for women; proper health and safety conditions; maternity leave etc.
>
> 2. It can protect you against victimisation.

3. It can negotiate with your boss about pay, hours of work and holidays.

4. It can offer help and advice with benefits, National Insurance, etc.

Shop stewards are the union representatives in the work place and they are elected by their work mates. When you start work, find out who they are because a shop steward is the person to go to if you have problems.

It's not only people in industry who need the protection of Trade Unions. Teachers, nurses, office and shop workers have all formed themselves into unions. Even university professors have a union!

Let's look now at some of the problems that you may face at work. There's an old saying that goes 'forewarned is forearmed' meaning that if you know about something in advance you're more likely to be able to do something about it. In the work place ignorance is never bliss.

RIGHTS AT WORK

Everyone in work, either full-time or part-time, is legally entitled to certain basic rights. They are known as statutory rights and they are the result of various acts of parliament.

You have the right:

- not to be discriminated against on the grounds of race
- not to be discriminated against on the grounds of sex or marriage
- to equal pay for equal work
- to minimum pay and employment conditions
- to a safe system of work
- to belong to a trade union
- not to be unfairly dismissed

You also have the right to
- an itemised pay statement
- payment in cash
- notice of termination of employment
- to pay when laid off
- to redundancy pay
- to written reasons for dismissal
- to statutory sick pay
- to time off to serve on juries, for Trade Union activities etc
- to maternity benefit
- to a written contract

Most employers abide by the law and hopefully you shouldn't have to get involved in disputes over your rights. Unfortunately there are a minority of employers who don't and who rely on their workers' ignorance of the law and their rights to take advantage of them.

Don't be an ignorant worker!

Know your rights *before* you start work. Otherwise you could end up unfairly dismissed, sexually harassed, underpaid or badly injured.

Within thirteen weeks of starting work you should be given a written statement of the main terms and conditions of your employment. This is your contract, although by agreeing to take the job offered you have already entered into a form of contract with your employer. There are two sides to the contract and they involve what you have to do as an employee as well as what is expected from your employer.

YOU will be expected to give good, faithful and honest service; to obey orders – as long as they are reasonable; to use reasonable skill and care.

YOUR EMPLOYER will have to take care of your health and safety at work and stick to agreements on wages, hours and conditions of work. Your written statement should include:

>your name
>your employer's name
>the date you started work
>the name of the job
>how much you earn
>how often you're paid
>how many hours you work
>what time you start and finish
>what your holidays are

what sort of notice you have to give or be
given
what to do when you're sick
details about pension arrangements
company rules and regulations
who you can complain to if you have a
problem

If, at your interview, or in the advertisement
for the job, it was stated that you would be
given some form of training, then this should
also be included in the terms of the contract.
If it isn't, find out why not. As a young worker
starting out on a job or career you have exactly
the same rights under the law as someone who
has been working for thirty years. But there is
lots of evidence to show that even with the law
on your side, bosses, and sometimes even fellow
workers, will try to deny you these rights.

Wherever you work and whoever you work
with, you may at some stage in your working
life come across discrimination, racism, sexism or
contraventions of health and safety regulations.

Sexual Harassment

Most young women find themselves at the
receiving end of some form of sexual harassment
at some point in their lives. By the same token a
lot of young men are guilty of sexually harassing

them, although they may think of it as teasing. You've probably seen it happening at school – a gang of boys standing round making suggestive or insulting remarks about particular girls – usually related to their supposed sexual exploits or to the size of a particular part of their anatomy!

Some of this behaviour might seem harmless enough, like being whistled at (or whistling) in the street. It's also so commonplace that you might wonder what's different about it when it happens at work.

The difference is that at work this behaviour is now recognised as sexual harassment and you have the right to protection from it. Of course, boys and men can also experience sexual harassment (from women or from other men) although it's rarer.

Sexual harassment covers a variety of behaviour:

- Embarrassing jokes or remarks – of the 'lovely pair of knockers' or 'There was this little tart . . .' kind, usually accompanied by a lot of nudge nudge, wink wink behaviour. When people (usually men) carry on like this all the time it can be very annoying and very wearing.
- Unwelcome comments on dress or appearance – when I first started teaching women were not supposed to wear trousers to work.

The explanation given by the male deputy head was that it was because the men liked to see our legs! Times have changed, I hope, but remarks about your dress can still be out of order.

- Unwanted physical contact – the obvious one is having your bottom patted or pinched but it can take lots of forms and actually count as assault under the law. Certainly if somebody gets hold of you and tries to kiss you or grope you without your consent they are guilty of assault and possibly indecent assault. Rape is an extreme form of sexual harassment.

- Demands for sexual favours – sometimes people. are offered promotion or better working conditions in exchange for sleeping with the boss – or threatened with the sack if you don't.

- Pin-ups and pornography – if you work in a place where your colleagues are mainly men, in a factory or a garage perhaps, there will often be displays of pictures from 'girly' magazines of a more or less explicitly sexual nature. Lots of women find these offensive. In many offices pin-up calendars are on the walls and are even sent out by some firms as part of their publicity.

If you encounter any of these things and

you feel upset, threatened or humiliated as a result, you are being sexually harassed. Because men usually have the power in the workplace they think that they can get away with it but you don't have to put up with it, even if it's your boss who's doing it. If you're a boy and you're being harassed, you shouldn't put up with it either.

You should:

- Keep notes of when and where it happens and who's responsible.
- Talk to your colleagues and see if they have had the same experiences.
- Talk to your trade union representative – the unions have policies against sexual harassment and will take up your case for you.
- If necessary you can go to the Citizens Advice Bureau or even consult a lawyer.
- Above all you should not tolerate it.

Don't be afraid of confronting the person responsible or of reporting it:

- If you are threatened with the sack your employer would be guilty of unfair dismissal and can be taken to court.
- Go to your boss or manager (unless they are the ones harassing you!) and ask them to speak to the person involved.

- Talk to your colleagues and get their support.
- Whatever happens don't feel that you have got to give up your job because of it – you aren't guilty of anything!

It's important for boys and young men to be aware of how unpleasant it is to be sexually harassed. It sometimes happens to them – perhaps if they're the only young man working with a lot of women – the post boy in an office, a messenger in a factory, or a similarly powerless position. It usually takes the form of non-stop teasing, although it can be more physical, but it can make life hell in the same way as it can for girls/women. Another form of sexual harassment young men can suffer is during 'initiation ceremonies' sometimes performed in the armed services or the fire brigade. These often involve subjecting the young recruit to a series of humiliating sexual 'jokes'. The less macho the person involved the more cruel the 'jokes'.

Of course, for this sort of behaviour to stop completely it would need a huge change in the way sex roles are seen in our society.

Sex Discrimination

Sex discrimination is when you are put at a disadvantage simply because of your sex. It may or may not be related to sexual harassment, and it can apply to both men and women.

Sex discrimination may mean that you are paid less or have less chance of promotion. It may mean that certain jobs are barred to you simply on the grounds of your sex.

At school it may mean that you are not allowed to take certain subjects because they are associated with the opposite sex – girls may be actively discouraged from taking metal work, Craft, Design and Technology or car mechanics, boys may be barred from Child Development or typing. On youth training schemes girls are often discriminated against. Nearly two thirds of all girls are concentrated in community service areas and offices. Only 3% of trainees at skill centres are female.

Like sexual harassment, sex discrimination is something that women and girls suffer from more than men and boys and the most effective way to alter the situation is to try and change people's attitudes to gender roles.

The law states that if a woman is doing the same, or broadly similar, work to a man and they are both working for the same employer then she is entitled to the same rate of pay and terms of employment as that man.

This applies to all sorts of work. For many years women in certain jobs were paid less than men for doing the same work because the men were considered to be the 'breadwinners', and their work was seen as more important. Women were considered to be working for 'pin money', that is money to buy a few luxuries or extras. But increasingly women have had to become breadwinners too. (And of course, there were always families for whom the woman's wage was the only source of income or was just as vital as that of her husband if the family were to survive.)

Even in jobs where the pay was the same for men and women (such as teaching and the Civil Service), women were often not promoted but left on the lowest rung of the careers ladder because they might marry and have children. In fact, whether you intended to have children or not was quite a common question to women at job interviews. Until very recently certain well known firms were even questioning women job applicants on their periods! Men never get asked such personal questions and have *you* ever heard of a man being turned down for promotion because he is likely to become a father?

Things are getting better though. Your generation is certainly less likely to suffer from discrimination against women, but old habits die hard and it's still a struggle for many women as these recent cases show:

'LAW LORDS REJECT FIRM'S BID TO BLOCK EQUAL PAY FIGHT'

In this case, five women working in a mail order firm as warehouse checkers had to take their case for equal pay with their male colleagues as far as the House of Lords before they could even take it to an industrial tribunal.

'EQUAL PAY FOR WOMAN TEACHER'

Here a woman who was supervising school leavers on a youth training scheme went to an industrial tribunal because a man doing the same job was being paid £270 a year more.

'SEVEN YEAR FIGHT FOR EQUAL PAY'

In this case a woman cook at a ship yard in the North of England claimed that she deserved equal pay with male craftsmen who earned up to £25 a week more than she did. She claimed that her work was as skilled and the conditions she worked in as unpleasant, as that of the men.

Men can claim sex discrimination too:

'MAN WINS SEX BIAS CLAIM'

This is the case of a man who was awarded £450 by an industrial tribunal as compensation for the 'upset and injury caused to his feelings' when he was turned down for a job because the firm wanted to attract more women workers.

As far as women are concerned the other main aspect of discrimination is in access to jobs. The idea that you have men's work and women's work is still widespread. It is uncommon enough to make the national and local press when women break into traditionally 'male' areas of employment, such as train driving, oil exploration and deep sea fishing. It still causes stares, not to mention rude remarks about female drivers, when you have a woman bus driver.

Women's hourly earnings are still only 75% those of men.

Women are still only a tiny minority of those holding top jobs – judges, senior civil servants, managing directors, university professors – in spite of the fact that we have had a woman prime minister for the last decade!

When you start work, if you think you are being discriminated against, you should talk to your employer or manager and get advice from your trade union. If that doesn't work you can ask for advice from the Equal Opportunities Commission or from the Advice, Conciliation and Arbitration Service (ACAS). If your employer still refuses to recognise your rights then you can go to an industrial tribunal. The Equal Opportunities Commission will give you free help and advice if they think you have a good case as they will if they think you have been refused a job on account of your sex.

Remember, the law is on your side.

Racial Discrimination

Just as it is now illegal to discriminate against someone because of their sex, it is no longer legal to treat people differently on the grounds of their race. But of course it still happens, and for much the same reasons. Attitudes take a long time to change. They lag behind changes in the law, especially in a society like ours where prejudice is common and racist jokes and behaviour are seen as a 'normal' part of everyday life by many people.

The Race Relations Act 1976 says that it is against the law to discriminate against people on the grounds of their colour, race, nationality or ethnic and national origins.

Discrimination can be:

DIRECT – when someone is treated less

favourably than others on racial grounds, eg not getting a job because you are black.

INDIRECT – when conditions are applied that affect a particular racial group more than others but cannot be justified on non-racial grounds, eg refusing to let Sikh bus drivers wear turbans.

It's also against the law to victimise someone, say by sacking them, who has complained about being discriminated against.

If you are a member of an ethnic minority group or you work alongside people who are, you should know that it is against the law for employers to discriminate on racial grounds:

- in the way they advertise and interview for jobs
- by offering less wages or poorer conditions
- by refusing to employ someone because they are from an ethnic minority group

Once a member of an ethnic minority group has been employed it is against the law for them to be treated differently:

- in terms of wages, hours of work or duties to be done
- in terms of opportunities for training and promotion
- by unfavourable or unfair treatment

If you experience discrimination when applying for jobs or at your work place, or you know anyone who does, then help can be got from the

Equal Opportunities Commission. It's the same sort of procedure as for sexual discrimination and you may qualify for compensation, as in the following examples:

> *United Biscuits had to pay out £48,507 to three Egyptian employees for unlawful racial discrimination and unfair dismissal.*
>
> *A security firm had to pay a black security officer £2,416 for having discriminated against him on racial grounds. In this case he had been dismissed for having 'unsatisfactory' references.*
>
> *£3,382 was paid to a sales assistant who was passed over for a job because she was black.*

There are hundreds of such cases still every year. And it's not only after you leave school and look for work that the trouble starts.

Two pupils of West Indian origin were refused work experience placements in a local electrical repairs company because they were black. The manager said that his work force would not accept them.

In one area with a 15% ethnic minority population not a single Asian or West Indian young person was recruited by the major high street stores.

Once you are at work you may experience racist remarks and jokes made by your colleagues. We're all familiar with 'Paki' jokes and Irish jokes and lots of people who would be upset if they were called racist still laugh at them. It's really important for those of you who aren't part of an ethnic minority to challenge such jokes and remarks – both at school and at work. It's only by trying to change people's attitudes through education and discussion – and your own example – that things will be improved.

Unfair Dismissal

Of course, not all unfair dismissal is on racial or sexual grounds. There are other reasons for giving you the sack which are still considered unfair by the law:

- If you are dismissed because of trade union membership or activity
- If you are dismissed because you are pregnant, although you are still able to do your job
- If you are dismissed because your employer is moving his/her business.

The law entitles you to be treated fairly by your employer. Employees must have a valid reason for dismissing you and they must treat you reasonably.

It's worth knowing the reasons for which you can be *fairly* dismissed as well. It's up to you as a worker to make sure that you don't provide your boss with a reason to sack you!

You can legally be dismissed for the following reasons:

- conduct – which could include dishonesty, poor timekeeping, rude or uncooperative behaviour
- capability – if you are genuinely not up to the job and don't have the necessary qualifications
- statutory reasons – for example if you work as a driver but lose your driving licence.

There might also be a case for fair dismissal if you've been involved in a criminal offence or if you've been absent for long periods.

If you are made redundant, which means that there is no longer any work for you to do because the firm has closed down or has had to shed part of its work force, it can be fair or unfair. It's not the same as being given the sack because it's not your fault, and it certainly shouldn't be held against you by any future employer. You should also receive some redundancy payment. If you are chosen for redundancy because you are in a union, or are a woman then this may be seen as unfair dismissal.

If for whatever reason you think you have been dismissed unfairly then you have the right to take your case to an industrial tribunal. Sometimes you needn't go so far. Your union representative may argue on your behalf and persuade your employer to take you back. There have been lots of cases where people have gone on strike in support of union members who have been unfairly dismissed.

Some Points to Remember

- You can't be sacked out of hand unless you've done something really wrong – been caught with your hand in the till, for example.
- If you've been working for more than four weeks you are entitled to a week's notice. This means you can carry on working for another week after you've received notice of dismissal. Sometimes it suits both sides if you take a week's pay in lieu of (instead of) notice.
- You should never be sacked without being warned – if you come in late for example, or are rude you should be given a chance

to improve before you are sacked.

- If you are sacked, ask for the reasons in writing – it's your legal entitlement if you've been working somewhere for more than six months.
- Always tell your union if you consider the sacking to be unfair, or if you're not in a union, go to the Citizen's Advice Bureau.

Health and Safety

You might think that going to work is as safe as houses BUT each year over 500 people are killed and more than 400,000 injured at work (nearly 19,000 in the construction industry alone) – so much for as safe as houses!

The awful thing is that most of these accidents are avoidable. They are the result of carelessness, bad planning, inadequate safety regulations, and sometimes negligence on the part of employers who are more concerned with making a fast buck than ensuring a safe working environment.

The types of accident range from dramatic and horrifying happenings such as the explosion on the Piper Alpha oil platform in July 1988 in which 166 men died in a blazing inferno, to daily occurrences of backstrain from badly positioned VDUs.

In between are the people suffering from

chronic breathing problems caused by working in coal mines, or with asbestos.

Some jobs are particularly dangerous in themselves – working high on scaffolding, working underground, working with radio-active materials, and some carry with them the real likelihood of being killed or injured – such as the armed forces. On the whole people going into those sort of jobs know there are risks attached. But even routine office and factory jobs have their dangers.

Every year more than 5,000 serious injuries occur in offices, and these are only the ones that get reported. They are caused by faulty electrical equipment, unguarded equipment like guillotines and by general over-crowding. In the catering industry people suffer burns, cuts and scalds, and in the manufacturing industry more than 59,000 injuries are reported each year of which 117 are fatal.

And it's not just when you start work that you are in danger. On work experience and youth training schemes you may be even more vulnerable.

Now, I don't want to frighten you BUT:

> over 30 young people have been killed and over 1,000 suffered major injuries while working on Youth training programmes

since 1980. This is partly a result of their own inexperience and lack of training, but occasionally the result of negligent or careless employers' failures to provide proper safety equipment or supervision.

As a young person under eighteen there are a whole range of industrial activities which are forbidden you by law simply because of their potential danger. For example, you are not allowed:

- to operate cranes and lifting appliances on building sites
- to test electrical circuits above 50 volts
- to operate certain woodworking machines
- to set up tools on power presses
- to work at a chrome plating bath
- to work with radio-active substances
- to work in an off-shore installation

In fact, there are thirty-five categories of work considered too hazardous for young people. There's also a long list of machines including dough mixers, garment presses, power presses, potato chipping machines, circular saws and wooden turning lathes that young people should not be allowed to work on unless they've had proper training and are adequately supervised. You should never be expected to clean or maintain any machines of this kind.

There are all manner of horror stories connected with young workers and industrial accidents:

- a sixteen-year-old boy dragged into a bag flattening machine and killed
- a trainee dying of massive head injuries while operating a paper baling machine
- three fingers cut off by a guillotine . . .

As I said, I don't want to frighten you. Such accidents shouldn't happen – they could all have been prevented and the law is very definite about what employers should do to ensure their workers' safety.

The Health and Safety at Work Act 1974 is designed to protect people at work and it is the employer's duty to provide this protection by:

- maintaining a safe plant and safe systems at work
- ensuring the safe use, handling and storage and transport of articles and substances
- providing adequate instruction, training and supervision
- maintaining safe premises
- providing a safe working environment and adequate welfare arrangements
- All employers of five or more workers must have a written safety policy and their employees must know what it contains.
- All protective clothing necessary for a job, be it hard hat, overalls or ear muffs, must

be provided by the employer.

But as a worker you're expected to take some responsibility as well:

- You must take reasonable care to avoid injury to yourself or others and cooperate with your employer in meeting safety requirements.
- If you're provided with protective clothing but don't wear it because you can't be bothered or don't fancy the way you look in it, then it's YOU who are guilty of breaking the law.

Let's look at what this means for you in the work place – and remember this applies just as much if not more, to work experience and youth training schemes as well as to full employment.

There are various laws that protect you at work including the Factory Act and the Health and Safety at Work Act. They apply to such things as fire regulations, the state of the toilets and kitchens as well as to the safety of machines and processes.

Each work place should have:

- a copy of the Health and Safety at Work Act
- clearly visible fire instructions
- an accident book
- a health and safety representative
- some basic first aid equipment

If you're working with potentially dangerous

equipment or substances then protective clothing should be provided.

When you start work you should be given information about health and safety procedures and about sick pay and compensation. You should also be given proper supervision until you are experienced and confident enough to work on your own.

You must have a responsible attitude to safety yourself – be careful, use the safety equipment, don't take short cuts, don't play with machines, don't sample substances or check power sources. Keep away from moving parts . . . If you think you are being expected to work in unsafe conditions, report it to your health and safety rep. or your shop steward.

If you have an accident, report it. If it's not your fault you are entitled to compensation although this might be quite difficult to get, especially if you contract a disease rather than do something more dramatic like cut off your hand!

Remember there are quite a few work places where there is no union representation and where the work conditions are pretty awful – garment making 'sweat shops', the catering industry, some construction sites, some garages, some offices.

ASK about conditions and precautions when you go for an interview. The majority of employers abide by the law and provide reasonable working conditions for their employees and if they don't, you have the law on your side.

You may well be feeling that none of this is likely to apply to you. Perhaps you are a young white man, hoping to go to university and then follow a career in the law or in advertising. But you could still find yourself caught in a fire at work and not able to find your way out of the building because there are no fire notices, or you could be injured in a badly maintained lift. A safe working environment is even more important if you are a young Asian woman who may end up working in a sweat shop with old and dangerous machines to produce cheap clothing.

If we consider the four school leavers in chapter three, we can see that they could all potentially suffer from the denial or neglect of their rights.

Ayesha could be sacked from her office job as a computer operator because she is pregnant; Susan may never be more than a Junior doctor because medicine is one of those professions where it is notoriously difficult for women to get promoted into senior positions; Sean could have a serious accident working for a cowboy builder who ignored safety regulations, and Winston may find himself being turned down for jobs because he is black.

If this chapter has seemed a bit like a lecture on do's and don'ts at work it's because it really is important that you know about your rights and those of others. They apply to everyone from a managing director to a McDonald's counter hand, so don't be afraid to stand up for them!

POSTSCRIPT

I hope this book has given you some ideas to help you start thinking for yourself about what you want to do with your life – not just in terms of your paid employment but in other aspects as well: leisure, friends, family life, interests, involvement. . .

One of the main things I hope you will have realised is that a lot of what will happen to you is up to you. Of course there are some things which you will be powerless to influence but on the whole it's the choices that you make yourself which will shape your life.

I've deliberately not said much about actual jobs. That's the next stage, and that's up to you. Good luck!

FOLLOW UP

USEFUL ADDRESSES

The following organisations produce a range of material, much of it free, which they will send you on request. It will be useful for extra background on many of the areas dealt with in this book.

Training Commission
Moorfoot
Sheffield S1 4PQ
– information on all aspects of work and training

Careers and Occupational Information Centre (COIC)
Moorfoot
Sheffield S1 4PQ
– all aspects of careers information

Careers Research and Advisory Centre (CRAC)
Bateman Street
Cambridge CB2 1LZ
– all aspects of careers information

Prince's Youth Business Trust
8 Jockey's Fields
London WC1R 4 TJ
– for help in setting up in business if you are
young and unemployed

Trade Union Congress
Congress House
Great Russell Street
London WC1B 3LS
– trade union history, rights at work, health
and safety etc.

Equal Opportunities Commission
Overseas House
Quay Street
Manchester M3 3HN
– information on all aspects of equal oppor-
tunities especially sex discrimination.

Commission for Racial Equality
Elliot House
10-12 Allington Street
London SW1E 5EH

– information on race relations legislation

Advisory, Conciliation and Arbitration Service
(ACAS)
Head Office
11-12 St James Square
London SW1 4LA
– information on unfair dismissal, rights at work
etc.

National Council for Vocational Qualifications
(NCVQ)
222 Euston Road
London NW1 2BZ
– information on all vocational qualifications

Voluntary Service Overseas (VSO)
9 Belgrave Square
London SW1X 8PW
– information on voluntary work abroad

Community Service Volunteers (CSV)
237 Pentonville Road
London N1
– information on voluntary work in Britain

Health and Safety Executive (London)
1 Long Lane
London SE1 4PG

– information on all aspects of health and safety at work. (See also regional HSE addresses in local phone books.)

There are also places in your own locality where you will be able to get useful information:

The Job Centre
The Department of Social Security
The Citizen's Advice Bureau
The Reference Library
The Post Office
The Further Education College

USEFUL BOOKS

Your school library and your local library will have a wide variety of books about different jobs and your Careers teacher or Careers Officer will be able to give you lots of specific information. And, of course, you can always write off for information to various firms and organisations yourself. Here are just a handful of general books that you might find useful:

How to Get That Job
Joan Fletcher
Northcote House Publishers, 1987
ISBN 07463 0326 2

Unqualified Success
Juri Gabriel
Puffin Books 1984
ISBN 014 031288 9

The Daily Telegraph Careers A–Z
Careers Intelligence
Collins 1988
ISBN 0 00 434 150 3

The Alternative Careers Book
eds. Klaus Boehm & Jenny Lees-Spalding
Papermac 1988
ISBN 0 333 46580 6

Careers and Jobs Without O Levels
Thelma Barker
CRAC, 1986
ISBN 0 86021 890 2

How to Choose a Career
Vivien Donald
Kogan Page Ltd 1986
ISBN 185091 097 9

What Colour is Your Parachute?
Richard Nelso Bowles
Ten Speed Press,
California 1988
ISBN 0 89815 176 7

Your First Job
Ann Page
Kogan Page Ltd 1984
ISBN 0 850 38 485 0

Be Your Own Boss at 16+
Alan S. Watts
Kogan Page Ltd 1986
ISBN 1 85091 041 3

Job Hunting For Women
Margaret Wallis
Kogan Page Ltd 1987
ISBN 1 85091 241 6

Employment for Disabled People
May Thompson
Kogan Page Ltd 1986
ISBN 1 85091 127 4

The Student Book
eds. K. Boehm, Nick Wellings,
Jenny Lees-Spalding
Papermac 1988
ISBN 0 333 43565 6

The School Leaver's Handbook
Jacquie Hughes
Adamson Books 1986
ISBN 0 948543 000

Index